Persuading *for* Results

HOW TO BECOME A PERSUASIVE PRESENTER

Stephen Kozicki

Gary Peacock

TODD,

"FORTUNE FAVOURS THE BOLD!"

Stephen Kozicki

2012

C Peacock
2012

Bennelong Publishing

Practical tools and insights for Business Results

Persuading for Results

© 2011 Stephen Kozicki and Gary Peacock

This publication is designed to provide accurate and authoritative information in regard to the subject matter covered. It is sold with understanding that the publisher is not engaged in rendering legal, accounting, or other professional service. If legal advice or other expert assistance is required, the service of a competent professional person should be sought.

Published 2011 by Bennelong Publishing Pty Ltd, 2nd Reprint.
PO Box 500
St. Ives NSW 2075
Australia

Editors: Dani Little, Kate Dorrell, Philippa Watson and Rachael Kozicki.
Illustrations: Shana Grotenhouse.
Design: Anna-Louise Leonard and Dani Little.
Cover and text design, and page layout: DiZign Pty Ltd.

National Library of Australia Cataloguing-in-Publication entry

Author:	Kozicki, Stephen.
Title:	Persuading for results: how to become a persuasive presenter Stephen Kozicki and Gary Peacock; Editors, Dani Little … [et al.]; Illustrations, Shana Grotenhouse.
Edition:	1st ed.
ISBN:	9780980778809 (pbk.)
Subjects:	Public speaking. Self-presentation. Persuasion (Psychology)
Other Authors/Contributors:	Peacock, Gary. Little, Dani. Grotenhouse, Shana.
Dewey Number:	808.51

This book is distributed internationally through Bennelong Publishing Pty Ltd. The authors can be contacted at www.bennelongpublishing.com for further information or inquiries on conferences keynotes or workshops.

Dedication

This book is dedicated to the four most persuasive people that the authors know—our children, Rachael, Sarah, Hannah and Rebecca.

Foreword

As we navigate the 21st Century, there are more resources available to businesses than ever before. Yet, executives, senior managers, scientists, academics, researchers, and sales people still struggle to persuade groups, large and small. These professionals struggle to hold the attention of jaded and bored audience members, who have grown weary of a world over-stimulated by marketing and sales hype. *Persuading for Results,* the latest book by Stephen Kozicki and Gary Peacock, brings a new voice and a provocative perspective to the subject of how to persuade.

This book brings a timely perspective on how to get your message across in a discount-driven, time-deprived, access-constrained, hyper-competitive marketplace. Today, the new global competitive environment demands persuaders capture audience attention immediately, and then connect with each and every listener in the audience. Only then does the persuader's message break through the defences erected by seasoned business people to minimise marketing *noise*. Kozicki and Peacock provide the tools and methods to enable such breakthroughs.

Kozicki and Peacock offer concepts that are simple, but powerful. Moreover, Kozicki and Peacock share a *process* for developing and delivering compelling presentations—a *process* that almost anyone can understand and embrace.

This book cites examples from real presentations of successful persuaders, as well as previously unsuccessful persuaders. I can personally attest to the power of being mentored by Stephen Kozicki. His insights have assisted me in presenting on global marketing and business development issues throughout the world.

In short, *Persuading for Results* combines the formidable knowledge and experience of two knowledgeable persuaders, each with decades of experience persuading throughout the world. This book contains a road map to enable readers to fast-track their way to Persuading For Results.

Dr John A. Caslione
President & CEO
GCS Business Capital, LLC
Noted speaker, author and businessperson

John Caslione's latest best-selling book, *Chaotics, The Business of Managing and Marketing in the Age of Turbulence*, (www.chaoticsstrategies.com) with co-author Philip Kotler, offers insight and tools essential to navigate businesses through these uncertain times.

"*But what we all want and need is information we can learn and apply quickly. The work keeps on going; we don't have time to fool around.*"

Jefferson D. Bates

Acknowledgements

For their help and professional contribution we thank: Dani Little, Rachael Kozicki, Sarah McIntosh, Madeline Goldie, Philippa Watson, Kate Dorrell, Anna-Louise Leonard, Leigh Miller, Noa Olian, Jodie Cooper, Doug Burden, Vicky Karatasas, Craig Browne, Peter Houghton, Greg Stevenson, David Priddy, Karen Hood, John Leung and Ben Jolly.

For insight and inspiration: at AGSM, Professor Mark Hirst, Dan Lovello, Professor Robert Wood, Professor Geoff Eagleson, Nigel Bedford, Jane Bushaway, John Leung, Edwin O'Young, Paul Walshe and Tom Windeyer. At the Macquarie Graduate School of Business, Professor Ed Davis and Dr Allan Tidwell. Importantly, for his academic and practical business suggestions, Dr Siggi Gudergan, Assistant Dean Research Training and Head of the Management Discipline Group in the Faculty of Business and Law at the University of Newcastle.

We also wish to thank the many firms we have consulted for, groups and senior managers we have coached in persuasion skills and all the clients who have attended our workshops in Asia Pacific, Europe, United Kingdom and North America. Your generosity in sharing your experiences in many industries has helped us gain invaluable insight into the process of persuading for results.

As many people have helped us make a better book in this edition, if you see a quote or story without a proper citation and you know the source, please let us know.

Contents Summary

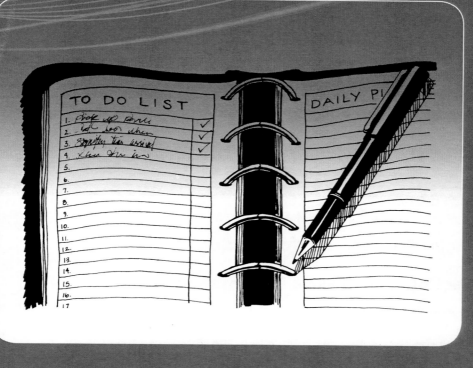

"Do less — but do it better."
Doug Burden

Contents Summary – Introduction

We have designed this book as a reference for fast and frequent use. We have also included this contents summary, so if you have a specific concern or interest, you can dive straight into the relevant Insight. We hope the summary will help you use the book in the way that is most effective for you.

Regardless of how you decide to use this book, the Introduction is vital reading because it introduces the models and case studies that appear throughout the book. If you skip the Introduction, you will have difficulty understanding the rest of the book. Two major case studies are used through the book, a business case for Colossal Sports and a sustainability case study in applying Permaculture to create a community garden.

....

Persuading for results takes more than just a thorough knowledge of your subject. It is equally important to communicate the information persuasively. Section 1 contains five Insights exploring the foundations and processes of persuasion. It will help you understand your current persuasion skills and how these skills measure up when persuading for results.

Section 2: Prepare To Persuade   39

Research and preparation are the keys to persuading for results. This section provides a step-by-step guide to researching and understanding the audience members and tailoring your presentation to meet their expectations.

Section 3: Style—Powerful Persuaders   **133**

In the words of James Humes, "the art of communication is the language of leadership."
This section looks at the practices of effective communications and explores ways that
you can use these methods in your own presentations.

Section 4: Style—Delivering Your Persuasion 199

With the preparation complete, it is time to move on to delivering your persuasion.

Section 5: Persuasion on the Run 221

In recent years, the standard of business presentations has improved. Now, small firms can present as professionally and impressively as large firms. To compete, The Persuasive Presenter must have a good command of technology. This Section looks at the future of presentations and helps you prepare.

Introduction

"I always skate to where the puck is going, not to where it has been."

Wayne Gretzky

When persuading for results, you will need to persuade individuals and to persuade groups. For most high–stakes persuasion, you must persuade a group—a group with diverse people, with diverse interests and with diverse opinions—this book will make you more effective at persuading groups.

When persuading a group, we recommend meeting some individuals alone to understand their interests, to understand their opinions and to influence them. For influencing individuals, we recommend Cialdini's book, Influence: Science and Practice, now in its fifth edition, which we summarise in Insight 5. Once you have influenced individuals, then to persuade a group to take action, a group of five or five hundred, our book shows you must be—a persuasive presenter.

Imagine this:

You have had a great week and as you settle back in your office chair to ponder the upcoming weekend, the telephone rings. Who could this be on a Friday afternoon? A social call perhaps? You pick up the telephone and discover it is the Managing Director. "You have been selected" she announces, "to be the lead speaker at next week's presentation." Your heart sinks as she says, "Remember this is our biggest potential client, ever."

As you hang up the telephone your heart rate increases and your mood sinks further. Not only have your weekend plans been shattered, but the future of the company is resting in your hands. How do you begin to plan the persuasion? How will you handle the pressure? How will you create a mind-blowing presentation?

If challenged, most people could list elements of a good presentation. They would mention the need to make presentations interesting, brief, informative and pertinent. Some people might also mention the value of good visuals and relevant examples.

If the elements of a good presentation are so obvious, why do most people panic when faced with a critical presentation? There are two reasons. First, common knowledge is not necessarily common practice. Second, there is a big difference between a 'good' presentation and a persuasive presentation. Unlike a 'good' presentation, a persuasive presentation will not be judged on its format, but on whether after the presenter's advice, the audience acted. This book will help you make the leap from good presentations to persuading for results.

We adopt a practical approach to helping readers make this leap. We understand the pressures facing budding (and seasoned) presenters, as they try to follow advice telling them to 'be confident', 'be funny', 'be authoritative', 'be clever' and above all 'be likeable.' No wonder people dread giving presentations to persuade.

Our approach to giving persuasive presentations is fundamentally different. Instead of giving glib tips on self-development, we take readers through a planning process that addresses every aspect of persuading for results. We are not concerned with presentations that aim merely to inform or entertain. We want to help you persuade for results: to become capable of influencing, inspiring and directing behaviour. So, we use a rigorous approach to planning and delivering persuasive presentations.

The other characteristic that distinguishes this book is its preoccupation with the audience. Most presenters focus on their content, seeking only to gather data and inform their audience. One of the most dangerous assumptions you can make is that the audience is passive. When Persuading For Results, you will present your content with the main objective to persuade your audience to take action — to buy an idea, to buy a product or to buy a service.

The following Persuading for Results Model© sets out the elements that we believe influence the outcome of persuasion. An insight into the audience is the foundation and it underpins the persuader's expectation for audience action. Only when you understand the audience and understand how your preferred action plan for the audience relates to the audience, can the persuader begin to plan a presentation.

Building on understanding the audience and identifying a preferred action, you can formulate a structure for the presentation. Balancing the content of the presentation with the style of delivery, you can prepare and deliver a presentation that persuades for results.

The Persuading for Results Model ©

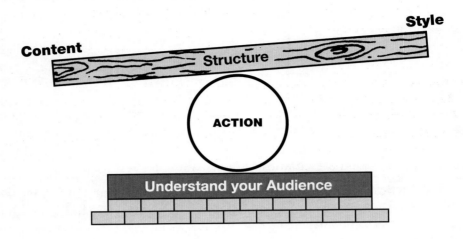

The Method

Before we go any further, we want to examine a successful presentation to help illustrate the way that various elements identified in the Persuading for Results Model© influence persuasion. With help from the former National Sales Manager for Bayer Animal Health, Doug Burden, we look at how a product launch presentation blew the competition away.

Bayer's Product Launch

Bayer is among the world's largest and most diverse companies with products ranging from plastics to agrochemicals. Bayer has been associated with innovation and research since its beginnings in 1863, as a three-man venture to manufacture synthetic dyes for the textile industry.

There are approximately 120 million sheep in Australia and over the years, Bayer Australia has developed products to increase the yield of their flocks. Some years ago, the need for a new treatment for lice was becoming urgent as the chemicals on the market were becoming less effective.

Bayer Australia launched Zapp, a new lice treatment. However, rather than just adding their noise to the clatter of industry marketing, Bayer executed a presentation that changed the industry's conception of a product launch.

From the start there was something different about Bayer's product launch. It was held in a historic wedding reception hall and sheep stood where the bride and groom normally stand for photographs. As people entered the hall they were visibly surprised. Some laughed out loud, while others wondered if they were at the right place. People were curious and excited even before the formal product launch began.

The technology behind Zapp was revolutionary and Bayer knew that it was vital that the audience, which was comprised of distributors, understood this. Bayer knew distributors would only sell Zapp to graziers if they understood and trusted the product. So, the presenter explained the science in detail and answered questions carefully and comprehensively.

The presenter then outlined a huge marketing campaign, involving in-store displays, brochures, technical notes and media advertising, to support the distributors in their sales role. This helped create a sense of opportunity and partnership.

At that stage of a standard product launch, a video is usually shown displaying how to use the product. However, this was no standard launch. The audience members were asked to move outside, where a dozen shorn sheep were waiting.

The guests were invited to test the application of Zapp on the live sheep, so they could see how easy it was to use. The distributors rolled up their sleeves and tested the product and asked the Bayer Technical Team many questions.

Doug Burden said, "The hands-on section of the product launch proved to be a hit. They absolutely loved it. I had people coming up to me after and saying it was the best product launch they had ever been to."

Zapp quickly surged to number one in its market. Zapp is still at the top years after the launch with over sixty percent of the market share.

The good news is that this success continued with Bayer's new product AVENGE™ which is the company's new pour-on sheep lousicide.

The launch of Zapp should challenge readers to re-evaluate their understanding of how to Persuade for Results in a group presentation. We want you to learn how to deliver ethical persuasive messages to inspire your audience to take the action you recommend, and how to produce sustainable results in business, your team, even your farm.

Some of the lessons from Bayer's message are clear, such as:

- Knowing your audience's needs and expectations *(Insight 8—Understand your audience)*.
- Carefully considering the venue *(Insight 40—Location)*.
- Involving your audience *(Insight 27—Involve your audience)*.
- Engage your audience by using different stimuli *(Insight 22—Visuals Add Value* and *Insight 36—Music and sound)*.

Major Case Studies for the Book

"Feed a man a fish and you feed him for a day,
teach a man to fish and you feed him for a lifetime."
Chinese Proverb

Major Case Studies

The first major case study for this book is a business case. However if you do not want to use the business case, we have also included a sustainability case study and invite you to use that to stimulate thought. Even if you do use the business case, we challenge you to use the sustainability case study to stretch your thinking and provoke new ideas.

We also hope it will encourage you to look for opportunities to persuade outside the business realm. Not only can you contribute to your community, but you can also practice your skills.

Case study 1: Colossal Sports

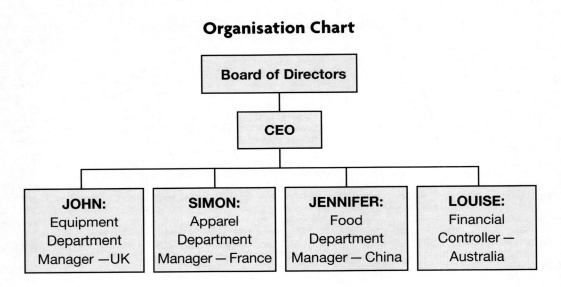

Organisation Chart

Colossal Sports is a large company, employing 300 staff, across three divisions, located on three different continents with a separate finance division. The divisions are Sports Equipment, Sports Apparel and Sports Food. The new five year strategic plan '15/5' has the goal of 15% growth in profits, year-on-year, for the next five years.

Sports Equipment Division

For the past decade, the Sports Equipment group has been the profit mainstay, accounting for 65% of company profit. For the future, Sports Equipment's sales are expected to increase only by inflation. John has presided over the Sports Equipment group for the past eight years and is proud of its solid record.

Sports Apparel Division

Simon manages the Sports Apparel group, which produces sport shoes, sport clothes and products such as sport towels, sport bags and drink bottles. The Sports Apparel group is significantly less profitable than the Sports Equipment group, and offers only modest growth in sales and profits. However, Sports Apparel products have a crucial role in overall company success because prominent sport stars wear Sports Apparel products.

Sports Apparel has a fantastic marketing team. Simon doesn't charge John to use Sports Apparel's marketing team and feels disgruntled when the Board of Directors fail to acknowledge that his marketing team spearheads the success of John's division.

Sports Food Division

Three years ago, Jennifer launched the Sports Food division, producing health food products for an increasingly health conscious population. Food produces good margins, but high set-up costs mean that Jennifer's line is not yet producing an annual profit. The Sports Food costs are heavily subsidized by the other divisions, which allow the Sports Food division to use their marketing teams and distribution channels at no cost.

Despite Sports Food being yet to generate a profit, its growth figures are high, and if growth continues at this rate, Sports Food will overtake Sports Equipment as the company's best profit division within ten years.

The Challenge

The CEO of Colossal Sports recently called the Financial Controller, Louise, into a meeting with the company's Board of Directors. The Directors were furious. They had just received the news that Colossal Sports had lost $300 million of business with Marbella Retailers.

Louise took a deep breath and explained that Marbella Retailers had cancelled their orders because Colossal Sports could not deliver the products on time. The Board demanded to know why they had not been able to deliver. Louise explained that Colossal Sports' supplier had put a credit stop on Colossal Sports, because of $200,000 in overdue invoices.

The CEO slammed his fist on the table and shouted, "Why weren't those invoices paid?" Louisa said, "Well, our current information system does not alert us to overdue invoices until 30 days after they fall due. Our supplier was patient for the first few times we were late, but it seems that we have been late with every invoice and their patience has run out. It is not anyone's fault. It is an information technology problem." The CEO stood up and said:

"Louise, this has cost Colossal Sports millions of dollars of business. This is not a technology problem. It is a management problem. We must achieve the goals of our 15/5 strategic plan—we want 15% growth in company profits year-on-year for the next five years. We cannot do this if we throw away key customers like Marbella.

I want a new information system within three months. I want a system that will tell us when our bills are due, not thirty days later. I also want a system that will tell me where the greatest profits are coming from, where costs can be cut, which groups are overstaffed and which groups are underachieving. I want a system that can track the performance of all managers, including you! You have three months to fix this or else you will be looking for a new job."

Louise contacted an information technology consulting firm and they created a blueprint for a new information system, which would provide the information the board wants. Louise now faces the challenge of persuading John, Simon and Jennifer to allocate funds from their budgets to implement the new information system.

John, Simon and Jennifer have heard the Board of Directors plans to use the new information system to track their performance. They are nervous and unwilling to let Louise decide which information system to implement. They think Louise will implement a system that gives data to make her look good.

The board gave Louise a mandate for a new system, but Louise will have to convince John, Simon and Jennifer her recommendation is the best one. She knows that this will be one of the most important presentations of her career.

As you read this book, you will join Louise at various stages of preparing and delivering her persuasive presentation to John, Simon and Jennifer. We will see her put many of this book's practical ideas into action. We will see her steer her way around serious roadblocks and learn from her experiences.

Case Study 2: Sustainability – Community garden

You may have bought this book to persuade others outside a business setting. Throughout the book you can take the templates and tools and apply it to a social example.

Many books, business and alike have challenged the authors to take action. For Stephen, one book that has a direct impact on his overall outlook is *Silent Springs* by Rachael Carson:

> **"The human race is challenged more than ever before to demonstrate our mastery — not over nature but of ourselves"**

This book started a journey that has evolved into doing something practical that will make a lasting impact on our ecology: Permaculture.

Permaculture was scientifically developed in Australia by Bill Mollison and David Holmgren during the 1970's. It is designing land-use to be sustainable based on ecological and biological principles. Permaculture often uses patterns that occur in nature to create stable, productive systems providing for human needs while harmoniously integrating the land with its inhabitants.

In a permaculture system the ecological processes of plants, animals, their nutrient cycles, climatic factors and weather cycles are all part of the picture. So work is minimised, "wastes" become resources, productivity and yields increase, and environments are restored. Inhabitants' needs are provided for using proven technologies for food, energy, shelter and infrastructure.

Geoff Lawton at www.permaculture.org.au describes permaculture as "working with, rather than against, nature", to minimise the need for energy outputs—be they human labour or mechanical/fossil fuel inputs. By creating energy-efficient and sustainable systems, human reliance on industrial systems—that Mollison describes as fundamentally and systematically destroying the earth's ecosystems—is reduced.

Permaculture principles can be applied to any environment, at any scale from dense urban settlements to individual homes, from farms to entire regions.

On a large scale, farmers would be encouraged to plant crops with a rotational cycle to enrich the soil with nutrients as opposed to mono crops, which deplete nutrients in the soil and eventually rendering the landscape barren. In Insight 35—Delivering Bad News, there is an example of dealing with issues of herbicides and pesticides and how this can affect the growth of farmer's crops.

At a community level, urban areas can establish community vegetable gardens to promote healthy and sustainable living and provide members with fresh organic produce. These gardens can also be used as public education centres for teaching permaculture principles and spreading the word for sustainable living.

Individuals and households can grow their own vegetables, install solar panels and insulation, re-use water, and introduce chickens to the system to reduce energy expenditure and waste. This system is not only sustainable, but also economical.

Throughout this book a hypothetical case study follows a keen permaculturist as she prepares to persuade her local council to allocate funds and a plot of land to build a community vegetable garden. After completing a Permaculture Design Course and researching the council policies, she has already gained support for the garden from members of the local community. Now, she has set up a meeting at council with key council members who will need to support the proposed community garden for it to be approved and the funds allocated.

This secondary case study shows how you can use the foundations of Permaculture to promote sustainable and healthy living within your local community, while showcasing how to use the Persuader's toolkit to persuade outside the business world.

> "What permaculturists are doing is the most important activity that any group is doing on the planet. We don't know what details of a truly sustainable future are going to be like, but we need options, we need people experimenting in all kinds of ways and permaculturists are one of the critical gangs that are doing that."
>
> Dr David Suzuki international environmental advocate.

If you decide to use a permaculture case study as your working example throughout the book, think about all of the different stakeholders involved. What would you do if you had to persuade the environmental authorities to take drastic action to solve the issue of food scarcity by creating urban community gardens? Or, what if you had the task of persuading angry farmers that using genetically modified seed damages the soil? How would you persuade chemical manufacturers to change their systems to minimize the flow of pollution into the waterways? As you work your way through the book, think about how you would use the tools provided to persuade for results about this or another sustainability issue.

Web Based Downloads

Using a case study as a working example will help you understand the process of persuading your audience and will show you how to use the presentation tools in the book. You will find blank copies of these tools at the end of the book and these can be photocopied and used when creating your own persuasive presentation. Alternatively, you can access the tools at **www.bennelongpublishing.com**. Use the login *persuading* with the password *results*. We will continue to add to the tools to ensure we always have the latest tools and ideas on the web.

Section 1
Persuasive Presentations

"What you say is common sense, but is it common practice?"
Australian Proverb

Insight 1
The Elements of Persuasion

'Let's compromise — we'll do it my way!'

Why do some people get other people's attention instantly, regardless of the environment or social setting? The history of persuasion shows that the ability to hold people's attention is independent of gender, appearance, age, social standing, educational qualifications or professional status. Some people just have natural charisma and the ability to persuade and influence other people. The rest of us need to develop these skills.

Persuasion, according to Plato, is the key to power. His student Aristotle wrote a book on the methods of persuasion called *The Art of Rhetoric* and recognised the skill of effective communication is indeed an art. Today, despite several millenniums of interest and writings on persuasion, people still struggle to be effective persuaders.

Aristotle identified three factors influencing communication: first *ethos*, which involves the characteristics of the **speaker**; second *pathos*, which is the emotional reaction of the **audience**; third *logos*, which is the logic of the argument, or the **content** of the message.

To develop the Persuading for Results Model© we considered four factors which influence persuasion. These are:

- The extent to which the presenter understands the needs and preferences of the **audience.**
- The **action** desired by the presenter.
- The **structure** of the message.
- The characteristics of the presenter: their **style and** their **content**.

Now is a good time to look again at the model and make sure you can identify the elements of persuasion that can be drawn from Aristotle. Specifically, ethos—concerning the characteristics of the presenter, pathos—concerning the response of the audience based on its unique composition, and logos—which involves both the structure and content of the persuasive presentation.

The Persuading for Results Model ©

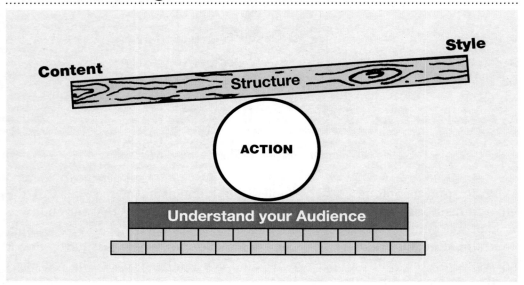

Take time now to examine the model and understand it. It will be referred to many times throughout this book. This model is new, but it draws inspiration from some of the greatest persuaders in history. If we look at some of the most persuasive speeches in history, we see the elements shown in the Persuading for Results Model.

Martin Luther King Jr's 'I Have a Dream' speech from the steps at Lincoln Memorial in Washington DC in 1963 is a good example of outstanding performance across the factors identified in the model. Let's take a closer look.

As a starting point, Martin Luther King Jr. understood the people in his audience. He understood their hopes, aspirations, fears and prejudices and he worked very hard to establish rapport. Throughout his persuasive presentation he identified with the **audience** by emphasising a common history and to some extent, common experiences. He engaged people from different racial backgrounds and urged them to adopt a shared dream.

To connect with the audience emotionally, he crafted the **content** of his message carefully. He filled his speech with vivid and emotive language. This created a sense of intimacy, anticipation and passion.

Martin Luther King Jr was a passionate advocate, who appealed to the emotions and ideals of his listeners. He did not say, "We should all be equal", he said, "We should be equal because it is written into The American Dream, we are all American and we were all created equal by God." He had the skill of crafting **content** that would alter the attitudes and behaviours of the audience.

There are many more examples of leaders who have effectively persuaded people for noble purposes. Nelson Mandela, for example, is also a captivating speaker.

Nelson Mandela learned early that persuasion was the key to action. In many parts of his autobiography *Long Walk to Freedom* he talks about improving his speaking and persuasion skills. Most would agree he is now a very persuasive presenter. This passage gives us a glimpse of the way he uses evocative language to reach his audience.

> **"I have walked that long walk to freedom. I have tried not to falter; I have made missteps along the way. But I have discovered the secret that after climbing a great hill, one only finds there are many more hills to climb. I have taken a moment here to rest, to steal a view of the glorious vista that surrounds me, to look back on the distance I have come. But I can rest only for a moment, for with my freedom comes responsibilities, and I dare not linger, for my long walk has not yet ended."**
>
> Nelson Mandela, *Long Walk to Freedom*.

Think of some of the world's greatest leaders and ask yourself, what makes their presentations so persuasive? They have different personalities, different ideas and different styles, yet their persuasive presentation styles have common attributes. They persuade by establishing their credibility, identifying with the goals of the audience, connecting with the audience emotionally and reinforcing their message through their content and style. Above all, a great speaker must be passionate about his or her topic—they must believe their message before anyone else will.

Insight 2
Presentation Preferences

"Know thyself."

Whenever a presenter stands before an audience, the presenter is judged. The observations of audience members vary, from the most complimentary comments, to the most cruel. While it might be tempting to ignore criticism of your presentation style, it is not going to help you improve. Instead, we hope to give you some insights into the different types of presenters, in the hope that you will start to recognise your own presentation preference. This is the first step to improvement.

There are different ways of analysing presentation styles. In recent decades, people such as Dr Carl Jung and Dr William Martson have dedicated themselves to learning more about persuasive communication and presentation skills. From the work of such people, emerged various models of communication, such as those based on a 'sender-receiver' paradigm, or the 'Mathematical Model of Communication', developed by Shannon and Weaver in 1949.

One of the weaknesses of many ways of thinking about, and teaching, persuasion skills is assuming people are clean slates, upon which a formula can be inscribed. Instead, we need to acknowledge that people come with a vast array of deeply embedded personality traits and strong presentation preferences. However, we also need to appreciate that all persuaders can improve their skills of presentation, and lift themselves into a better, stronger and more persuasive presenters. The first step to becoming a persuasive presenter is to face the hard truths about the limitations of the way you choose to present. Then it is possible to look at very practical ways to improve the outcome of your presentations.

Presentation Style Model

Our Presentation Style Model©, shown below for the first time in the book, depicts the balance between content and style. Indeed, how a presenter balances content and style will have a large impact on the audience's willingness to take action.

The model works on the premise that we all have preferences for how we like to present. The most persuasive presenters examine the context of the situation and decide the best and most effective style to use. Less persuasive presenters use their instinctive default preference in every situation, regardless of whether it is appropriate. We want you to be comfortable with all presentation preferences, so you can choose the most appropriate one for the given circumstances.

Let us begin by looking briefly at the four main presentation preferences—Persuasive, Entertaining, Technical and Basic. In the Presentation Style Model© below, the presentation preference is assessed according to **content** (what is being presented) and **style** (how the message is presented).

The Presentation Style Model©

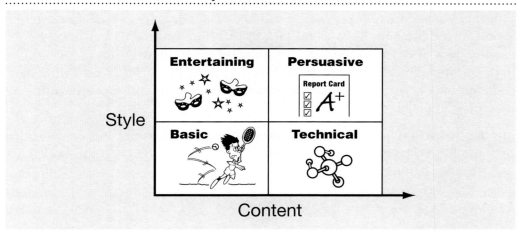

Your **style** is assessed according to how you deliver your presentation. Relevant factors will include the selection of visuals, use of colour, gestures, body language, nonverbal communication, personal appearance, music, humour, and other factors that comprise your personal style. The quality of your content is influenced by your research and your use of facts, figures, statistics and stories. An analysis of the model will reveal that a presenter with a persuasive style preference rates highly on both style and content.

Basic Presentation Preference©

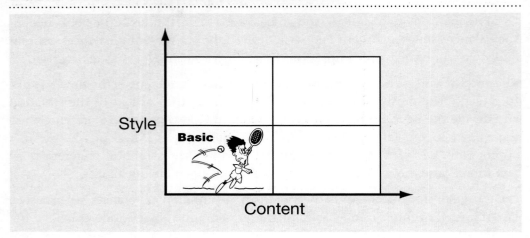

The basic presentation preference is characterised by low-grade content and a weak delivery style. This style is often boring and faltering or chaotic and rushed.

Some might argue that the basic presentation preference is not a preference at all, but simply the result of inexperience and nerves. We disagree. A basic presentation style is often the result of a wilful lack of planning (normally with a very good excuse), lack of research, laziness, unwillingness to try new things or a deliberate decision not to practise the presentation. The good news is that delivering basic presentations is not inevitable and this book will help you move beyond this presentation preference.

The basic presentation combines the lowest rating on both axes. However, two other presentation preferences can be almost as ineffective—the technical preference and the entertaining preference.

Technical Presentation Preference©

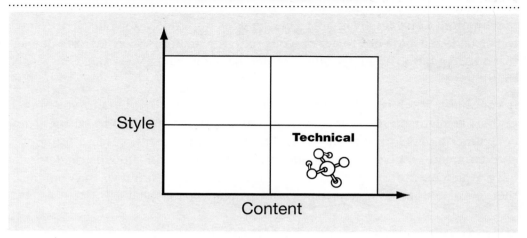

The technical presenter prefers comprehensive content delivery, at the expense of an engaging or interesting style. There are some positive elements of this preference. It is always important to have a good grasp of the relevant data, and sometimes it is necessary to devote much of the presentation to analysing specific information. However, this does not have to be at the expense of a powerful, persuasive style.

Data is usually used to inspire a response, and the way that you present that data will often influence the audience's response. A boring technical presentation has the potential to be as ineffective as a basic presentation, so this book will help technical presenters understand their preoccupation with content, and lift their style.

Entertaining Presentation Preference©

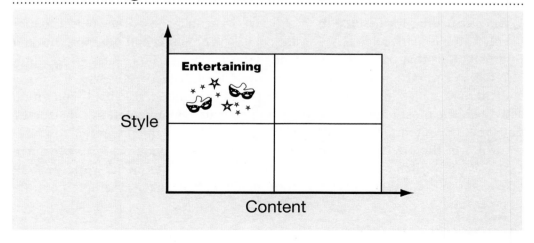

If you cannot be effective, at least be entertaining, right? Wrong. Consider the combined wages of your audience, who are not conducting business during your presentation. Consider the financial cost to your employer or to yourself, if you fail to persuade the audience to act on your recommendations. Consider the damage to your reputation if each audience member tells colleagues that you wasted their time.

If you are in the business world, but your sole aim is to entertain, you should find an amateur theatre company and sign up. When it comes to business, few companies invest in presentations merely for entertainment, because using only entertainment will persuade few audiences. This book will show persuaders who have a preference for entertaining presentations how to improve the content of their presentations, to match their existing high level of style.

Persuasive Presentation Preference©

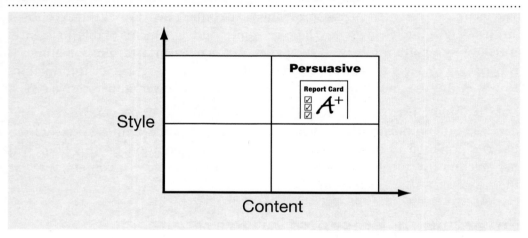

When Persuading for Results, the Persuasive Presenter knows the subject matter deeply and has marshalled the relevant data. This presenter can offer insights and interpretations that surprise and challenge the audience. The Persuasive Presenter also has a distinctive, creative and engaging style of delivery. This style keeps the audience enthralled, often by using colour, music, humour, visual aids and group activities. The most important feature of the persuasive presentation is balancing outstanding content and captivating style. Remember, as the presenter, you have control over the presentation and with the help of this book, you can become a Persuasive Presenter. Now that you understand the way the model works, we will take a close look at the four presentation preferences, using an example from the 21st century.

The Iraq Invasion

We chose to discuss the 2003 invasion of Iraq by the 'Coalition of the Willing', led by the United States of America, for several reasons. First, because the presentations by the world leaders about the prospect of an invasion were televised and it creates a reasonable context for discussion. So, many readers will recall seeing at least a few minutes of footage and will recall the rhetoric used to justify the invasion. Second, because the presentation preferences of several state leaders during this period provides a good opportunity to study the issues surrounding content and style, as seen on the Presentation Style Model©. Third, because both authors have a very strong view on the insanity of the invasion and how world leaders presented their cases for war.

At the United Nations (UN), one reason the 'Coalition of the Willing' did not gain the active support of a large portion of the world's leaders, was because they could not present their case for war persuasively. While President Bush Jnr. had managed to convince a deeply traumatised and grieving American population of the need of war, he could not convince a more critically thinking global audience. In particular his false claims about WMD's in Iraq, at the time were laughable by the rest of the world and after many inquiries were proven to be false.

The differing success of the persuasion attempts in the US and the UN are further illustrated by Prime Ministers Blair and Howard being unable to convince the majority of the people in the United Kingdom and Australia. Blair has since admitted that he pushed for the war,

even knowing it was unlawful because he wanted to maintain a close relationship with the US president. In fact, not dissimilar to the flawed reasons put forward by Howard. The majority of both countries were convinced the war was foolish and without moral or even legal justification. Both Prime Ministers did not understand that a critically thinking audience needs a more sophisticated method of persuasion. They both tried to use emotive lies to win over an audience, it didn't work then nor would it work now.

The lesson that President Bush Jnr. failed to learn in time, was a frightened national US audience would be easily convinced in the short term, but not in the long term. He also believed that by having over already 85% of the US population convinced of the invasion, he didn't need to be prepared. He was then and still is now a very basic and ineffective speaker particularly when he has an audience of critical thinkers.

Realising the UN Security Council members would not don their khakis in response to emotive rhetoric, Secretary of State Colin Powell finally varied the basic presentation style invoked by US leaders up until that time. Instead, Powell used the technical presentation style and made a highly technical presentation to the UN Security Council. However, doubts over the integrity of the data undermined this belated attempt to use data.

Despite world opinion splintering and people taking to the streets in the millions, these three failed leaders, Bush, Blair and Howard, did not waver from the rhetoric or repetition which had succeeded in persuading the US national audience. They made the mistake that many others have made before them—they confused being forceful with being persuasive.

Ultimately, the reason to go to war was for a regime change, it was to remove a brutal and deadly leader. Ironically and tragically, the decision to invade led to a succession of horrors, such as massive civilian casualties, the prison abuse scandal and the inability to preserve law and order.

Each of these horrors was subsequently invoked by terrorist leaders within Iraq to mobilise their own support, and, as history will judge with tragic results.

In contrast, we saw the example of the quietly spoken, but highly persuasive head of the UN weapons inspection team, Dr Hans Blix. Dr Blix used every opportunity to warn against the invasion of Iraq by invoking dramatic language, such as the phrase "there is no smoking gun", there are no WMD's combined with presenting compelling data.

Some might argue that he was not persuasive because the 'Coalition of the Willing' still invaded Iraq. Our proposition is quite different — his successful presentation meant that the rest of the world did not support the illegal invasion by the coalition of the willing.

History will be harsh on Bush Jnr., Blair and Howard, as their ultimate stupidity meant enormous suffering for the people of Iraq and the soldiers from the 3 nations who obeyed orders. The outcome now and in the future will be a democracy that will fail because of sectarian violence and inability to re-adjust to a post-war Iraq.

Even with the death of Osama Bin Laden in 2011, the violence in Iraq and Afghanistan continues to escalate with no end in sight.

Sadly, persuasion used with the sole purpose of manipulating audiences works and in this case with disastrous consequences.

Which style should you use?

The lesson from this example is that in some circumstances a basic presentation will be enough, particularly if your audience is almost convinced before you start speaking, or where the issue is not an important one. However, where the outcome of your presentation is important, and not a foregone conclusion, the best option is to use the persuasive preference.

Insight 3
Global Mistakes

Sign: "Wet Paint."
Question: "Why does everyone touch it?"

After discussing presenting to a global audience, it is worth mentioning the same mistakes are made by persuaders throughout the world. The most common mistakes are identified by Doug Malouf in the best selling book, *How to Create and Deliver a Dynamic Presentation* and by David A Peoples in *Presentations Plus*. As you read through this list, try to work out if you make these mistakes.

- Too much information
- Too much technical jargon
- Too long

- Not organised
- Not relevant
- Repetitive

Mistake 1 "Too Much Information"

Think about how you feel after a long family celebration lunch. After several hours of eating, many people can hardly move, have no energy, and feel like a big, bloated pudding. When you over-eat, your body focuses on digesting the mass of food in your system, to the exclusion of other activity. If you over-feed your brain, it has a similar reaction.

Keep this in mind when preparing your persuasion. If you give too much information, your audience will switch off. At the end of the presentation, their impression will be that your talk was boring or too heavy.

This problem is most characteristic of the technical presenter. If you feel this is reminiscent of your presentations, you should pay close attention to *Section 2: Prepare to Persuade*.

Mistake 2 "Too much Technical Jargon"

This problem began in the early 1990s during the computer boom. Boards and senior managers around the world were held ransom during technical presentations by their IT teams. Teams were able to present incomprehensible data and recommendations and get away with it. Today, the business community is far less tolerant of presenters who try to create a shroud of mystery and importance around their area of expertise by using jargon. If you need help to cut back on jargon and simplify your message, see *Section 3: Style—Powerful Persuaders*.

Mistake 3 "Too Long"

There are three possible reasons a presentation will go on too long. First, inadequate preparation, which leads to a rambling delivery of material. Second, not running question time effectively. Third, something is wrong with the equipment. Whatever the case, the presenter is at fault. There is no excuse for a presentation that goes over time.

Presentations that run over time usually come from technical or basic presenters. You will learn more about this in *Section 3: Style—Powerful Persuaders* and *Section 4: Style—Delivering your Persuasion*.

Mistake 4 "Not organised"

Speakers can be disorganised because of lack of structure or lack of preparation. Disorganised speakers do not know how to integrate material cohesively. Instead, they jump from one point to another without explaining the connection.

Disorganised speakers do not allow enough time to prepare. They throw material together at the last minute, without deciding what the main message is and without taking account of the audience's needs. They are guilty of the 'fill in time at any cost' syndrome and often have not prepared or checked visual aids before the presentation.

The bottom line is that busy people have no time to waste. A disorganised, rambling presentation will make them feel cheated and angry. So, if you are guilty of being disorganised—most likely a basic presenter—it is crucial that you read this entire book.

Mistake 5 "Not Relevant"

Your audience will usually expect to learn something new or be challenged to think in fresh ways. More often than not, an audience has come to you for something new, or insightful. Use old data and ideas at your professional peril.

How can you tell if your presentation lacks contemporary relevance? The alarm bells should sound when you hang on to a theory or theme that was popular five years ago or when you use language or examples that are out of step with the current business or cultural context. If you suspect that your ideas might need revamping, then every section of this book will help to inspire you with fresh ideas.

Mistake 6 "Repetitive"

Repetition can often be of benefit to the audience. When done in a subtle way, repetition reinforces a point, or relates an abstract point to a real situation. A pause, then a phrase repeated slowly and emphatically, can drive home a point. Repetition when done well can help persuade an audience.

However, when done poorly, repetition can bore an audience and destroy any chance of persuading them. If you suspect you may be repeating yourself, you will learn how to combat this problem as you read through the next section of the book.

Getting Better

These six mistakes are common and easy to make. However, do not panic because this book will help you avoid these and other pitfalls, through planning, preparing and practicing.

STEP	PREVENTS
Plan	Not organised.
Prepare	Too much information. Too much technical jargon. Not relevant. Repetitive.
Practice	Too long.

The purpose of starting this book with these common mistakes is to set you a challenge. If you make these or other mistakes, then you have the opportunity to learn a better way of creating and delivering presentations. If you want to Persuade For results, being aware of your mistakes is a good motivator. It will help you commit to a journey through this book, to commit to your goal to become a dynamic, effective, Persuasive presenter. So, let's get going.

Insight 4
Choosing Winning Frames

"People often confidently use frames that are outdated or plainly wrong to 'solve' their problems — with disastrous consequences. And too often a single view or thinking frame dominates our approach to everything. In complex situations it is rare that any single frame will be adequate."

Edward Russo and Paul Shoemaker

Windows of the mind

Imagine you have a house on a cliff edge. It overlooks the sea on the Eastern side and overlooks a lush green rainforest to the South. From the Eastern window, the sea dominates the view but in the bottom right hand corner of the window you catch a glimpse of the rainforest. From the South window, the rainforest fills the window with colour and birds and in the bottom left corner is a small square of sea.

Your task is to persuade a potential buyer to buy this house. You are only allowed to show the potential buyer the view from one of the windows. Which window will you choose?

When presented with this problem, people have three responses:

- Argue about the rules—"Why only one window?"
- Pick their favourite window—sea or rainforest.
- Ask questions about the purchaser.

Some presenters give similar responses as they try to persuade people:

- Argue about the rules—"That factor is not important."

- Pick their favourite window—"The most important thing is return on investment." or "The most important thing is people".
- Ask questions about the audience—"What are the most important things to the audience?" or "How do they see it?"

Sometimes it is useful to think of the audience as a buyer, because the audience needs to 'buy-in' to your presentation to take action. With the sale of the house, it is obvious which window you would choose for someone who sails and which window for someone interested in conservation. However the quotation at the beginning of this Insight reminds us that presenters often use outdated or inappropriate frames to persuade, with little success.

Frames guide our understanding and our options

> **Frames are the windows of our mind. They highlight some things and leave others in the shadows.**
>
> Russo and Schoemaker, Winning Decisions

Frames are tools we all use to simplify situations and guide our behaviour. Often we are not aware of these frames. These frames limit our view and limit the options we consider. Just like the windows in the house, they highlight some things and leave others in the shadows. Here are some examples of different frames:

ONE FRAME	ANOTHER FRAME
Cost	Investment
Purchase costs	Operating costs
Reduce costs	Increase profits
Reduce costs	Increase operating cash flow
Increase profits	Increase free cash flow
Increase profits	Increase return on investment
Negotiate on price	Negotiate on the relationship and the issues
Productivity	Job security
Production	Sales and marketing

When we speak to junior or senior people in various companies, we notice that they use different frames. Junior people talk about costs, while senior people focus on profit, and people who are even more senior might talk about cash flow and return on investment. Logically, a change in costs is closely linked to changes in return on investment. However, people are comfortable with their frames, and so if you use their frame your presentation will be more persuasive. The Persuasive Presenter aims to vary the frame according to the audience, and use multiple frames for a diverse audience.

People develop their frames over many years, and their frames are influenced by training and experience. People who spend all of their careers in operations have a different frame to those in sales. Similarly, a solicitor will have a different perspective to an accountant, as will a doctor and a nurse.

Losses and Gains

There is much research to support the idea that people generally have a strong aversion to losses. The Nobel Prize winner, Daniel Kahneman, and his colleague Amos Tversky, suggest people respond to challenges differently, depending on whether they are framed as losses or gains. Simply put, the pain of losing $100 feels much greater than the pleasure of gaining $100. Often people will make decisions to avoid losses rather than take the opportunity for gains. Any gain or loss is relative to a reference point, so part of the skill of framing is helping the audience choose a suitable reference point.

> **"It's not how rich you are that motivates your decision, but whether the decision will make you richer or poorer … As a consequence, … our preferences … can be manipulated by changes in reference point"**
>
> Peter L. Bernstein, *Against the Gods, the Remarkable Story of Risk.*

Imagine that you bought a house 10 years ago for $400,000. You estimate that the market value is $800,000 now and the house is on the market for $900,000. When you receive an offer of $700,000, is it:

- A $300,000 gain compared to the original price?
- A $100,000 loss compared to your target price?
- A $200,000 loss compared to your ideal price?

If you see it as a gain, you are more likely to accept the offer. If you see it as a loss, you are more likely to reject the offer. Remember, any gain or loss is **relative** to a reference point. Reference points can be the existing situation, a prior contract, a deal reached by a colleague or some level that you aspire to reach. When Persuading for Results, you will frame by suggesting a reference point that minimises losses and emphasises gains. If this is not possible, then help the audience understand the losses and propose some action.

Choose Frames Carefully

If you choose a winning frame, then the audience will often be unaware of how the frame is guiding their thinking. Framing is a powerful tool and when Persuading for Results you should use it ethically. Manipulating people to do things they later regret will not lead to long-term success. Our advice is, if you can not act with integrity then do not act at all.

Try Other Business Frames

In business, other frames provide different perspectives. Four useful frames are:

- Strategy Maps
- Four Types of Uncertainty
- Real Options
- Three Horizons of Growth

A Strategy Map is a tool for collecting four normally independent frames in one bigger frame. Kaplan and Norton developed the strategy map combining four frames: financial, customers, operations and learning. It is a useful tool for communicating with people who often only use one frame, because it shows how each frame links to the other and shows how the frames fit together to make the strategy work.

Uncertainty is increasing yet many of us were trained in techniques that assumed certain outcomes. We do not have good frames to cope with uncertainty and often simply describe issues as certain or uncertain. Hugh Courtney has developed a useful frame for uncertainty. He describes four levels of uncertainty in his book *20/20 foresight, crafting strategy in an uncertain world*. For each level of uncertainty, he identifies the most appropriate business tools.

On the subject of uncertainty, another powerful frame is 'Real Options'. Real Options is a frame that focuses on finding options that give businesses a high up-side and a low down-side. In uncertain environments, a portfolio of options allows a business to exercise only the options that are 'in-the-money', yet gives the flexibility to win over a wide range of outcomes. When you first discover the Real Options approach, it can be challenging and uncomfortable because it is so different to the frames commonly used. Some people will also be uncomfortable with the more mathematical aspects of this technique and would benefit from reading Martha Amram's introduction *Value Sweep: Mapping Growth Opportunities Across Assets*.

Another frame that can be useful in business is the 'Three Horizons of Growth'. Baghai, Coley and White provide a frame that classifies initiatives for growth into three categories and explains how each of these horizons requires different activities, different people, different systems and different management. Most businesses fail to achieve growth because they use a frame that is successful with today's business but is not effective to grow the businesses of tomorrow.

Learning to choose Frames

If you try to learn to frame in every possible way immediately, you are likely to get frustrated. If you accept that framing matters, then pick one kind of framing. For fourteen days listen and keep notes about that frame. Watch and listen to effective persuaders and ineffective persuaders. Ask people who seem to have a different view to explain the way they see things. Then, draft a small presentation twice, each framed in a different way. Remember that one kind of frame comes from metaphors or stories. Look at *Insight 34—Tell Stories* and try some different metaphors.

> **"Influence is a function of grabbing someone's attention, connecting to what they already feel is important, and linking that feeling to whatever you want them to see, do or feel."**
>
> Annette Simmons, *The Story Factor*, p 84.

Getting Better

The book *Winning Decisions* by Russo and Schoemaker has an extensive discussion of framing and recommends three steps:

1. Be aware of the frames you use.
2. Have more than one frame.
3. Use outsiders to get a different point of view.

Russo and Shoemaker recommend a practical way to implement these steps is to audit your frames and other people's frames:

AUDIT FRAMES TO GET BETTER...	
Highlights	What matters most to them?
	What do they talk about most often?
Shadows	What do I naturally consider that they rarely mention?
	What messages do they filter out?

Comparisons	How might others see this:
	In the same industry?
	In a different industry?
	In a different culture?
	What alternatives might you exclude that a colleague or a competitor might not?

Source: adapted from *Winning decisions*, Russo and Schoemaker.

Following is an example of how framing could be used in the Colossal Sports case study that was introduced at the beginning of the book.

FRAMING TOOL: COLOSSAL SPORTS

Ideas: Consider at least two different frames	**Frame 1: Growth** **Frame 2: Profit**
What does the frame highlight:	**Growth:** Highlights how Sports Equipment performed well in the past, but has little sales growth in the future. Sports Apparel offers modest growth, while Sports Food shows little profit at the moment but rapid growth of sales.
	Profit: Highlights that Sports Equipment produced good profits in the past, Sports Apparel is a lot less profitable than Sports Equipment, and Sports Foods is not profitable.
What is in the shadows of the frame:	**Growth:** Sports Apparel contributions to other divisions and company branding.
	Profit: Sports Apparel contributions to other divisions. Profit is currently only calculated at the company level, only sales and margins are calculated for divisions, total overhead costs are then subtracted to produce company profit. Currently division profits are estimated by allocating a percentage of the total overhead cost to each division. Therefore no one really knows what the profits of the divisions are.
	The other factor in the shadows of both frames is productivity—of financial assets and human assets. The company needs to produce a return on capital appropriate for the financial risk. Growth of sales and profits will only produce improved return on capital if the productivity of the financial assets is maintained or improved.
Comparisons—what are the differences	Growth is a positive frame for Sports Food and Sports Apparel but negative for Sports Equipment. In contrast, Profit is a positive frame for Sports Equipment and negative for Sports food.

FRAMING TOOL: COLOSSAL SPORTS (CONTINUED)

How can I frame to emphasise...	Emphasise gains	Minimise losses
Sports Equipment	**Growth**—Some growth of your profits will need to come from cutting costs because of slow future sales growth—this system will provide the details to help you control and cut costs. **Profit**—Show how much profit currently your division contributes to the company.	**Profit**—Will help avoid loss of big clients like Marbella. **Profit**—Will aid smart profit improvement by giving accurate information on costs to enable intelligent cost reduction rather than 10% reduction across all the division as in the past.
Sports Apparel	**Profit**—Will allow you to charge other divisions for services. Should give some recognition of the value added to other divisions.	**Profit**—Will help avoid loss of big clients like Marbella. **Profit**—Will aid smart profit improvement by giving accurate information on costs to enable intelligent cost reduction rather than 10% reduction across all the divisions, as in the past.
Sports Foods	**Profit**—Will help manage costs. One problem of rapid growth is managing expenses. The new system analyses expenses as a percentage of sales which is ideal for divisions with fast growing sales. **Growth**—One page summary reports will include growth of sales and growth of profit. This will ensure directors and managers see the sales growth and balance this against the poor current profits.	**Profit**—Will help avoid loss of big clients like Marbella. **Profit**—Will aid smart profit improvement by giving accurate information on costs to enable intelligent cost reduction rather than 10% reduction across all the division as in the past.

FRAMING TOOL: COMMUNITY GARDEN

Ideas: Consider at least two different frames	1. Build community spirit 2. Increase food security and nutritional health	
What does the frame highlight:	1. A need for a safe place that fosters the growth of food as well as acting as a meeting place. 2. Access to fresh nutritious food which ultimately lowers family expenditure.	
How can I frame to emphasise...	**Emphasise gains**	**Minimise losses**
Build community Spirit	Increased morale of community members. Increased sustainability of council parish. The large community group who support the garden are more likely to vote for you.	Approving the garden now will save you time discussing the issue with the large community group who support the garden. Approving will avoid the risk of losing the votes of this large community group.
Access to fresh nutritious food, lowered family expenditure	Healthier community. Creates a functional as well as social recreational area at minimal cost.	Will reduce some of the costs of handling rubbish because of increased recycling and composting.

Insight 5
Persuasion Produces Results

*"I like to think of sales as the ability to gracefully persuade,
not manipulate, a person or persons into a win-win situation."*

Bo Bennett

People lucky enough to travel to Paris often find that once they have worked out their sightseeing plan, there is limited time to see all of the museums, art galleries, fountains and churches. Unfortunately they might realise that they are only able to spend half a day at the Louvre Museum. Both authors have lost count of the amount of people who ask their advice on what to see as a "must do" in the museum.

Our answer is the same; you must see the "Mona Lisa" by Leonardo da Vinci.

Similarly, if you only have time to read only one book or research article on persuasion it would be by Cialdini, his Harvard Business Review article and his many books are the most cited references in virtually all other works on this subject. Robert Cialdini is Regents' Professor Emeritus of Psychology and Marketing at Arizona State University and his work is the foundation of most writing on persuasion. His book *Influence: The Psychology of Persuasion* has sold 2 million copies and has been translated into 26 languages. Also, Fortune Magazine listed it in "75 smartest business books".

In his Harvard Business Review Article, *The Science of Persuasion*, Cialdini introduces six tools of persuasion—practical and proven tools that work in many situations.

Bernie Madoff is currently serving 153 years in jail for one of the biggest financial scams in the world. It is estimated the amount missing from client accounts is a staggering $65 billion. Federal investigators believe the fraud started back in the 1980s and ran until 2008 when it was discovered. How could someone be so persuasive for more than 20 years and get so much money from so many smart and wealthy people?

In brief, Bernie Madoff used every one of the six tools and Cialdini's website (www.influenceatwork.com) discusses some aspects of the case. We mention this well-known fraud to show the power of these tools because it is interesting to analyse how some con men and criminals use these tools. However, we strongly recommend you only use these tools ethically and do not use them to persuade people to do things that they would not otherwise do. The table below summarises the tools.

CIALDINI'S SIX TOOLS	
Like	People like people who are similar to them. Look for similarities.
Reciprocity	People feel obliged to repay gifts and favours.
Social Proof	People follow the lead of other similar people. Use peer power when you can.
Consistency	People align their behaviour with small commitments. Make their commitments active, public and voluntary.
Authority	People defer to experts. Expose your expertise; do not assume it is self-evident.
Scarcity	People want more of what is rare or scarce. Highlight unique benefits and exclusive information.

When we work with clients, they often ask us similar questions about the tools and so the table below summarises their common questions.

COMMON QUESTIONS ABOUT CIALDINI'S SIX TOOLS	
How do they work?	We have less time to deal with complexity and so we use shortcuts to simplify decisions. These shortcuts work well most of the time but leave us open to occasional, costly mistakes.
Do I have to use all of them?	No, however the more tools you can use the more chance you have of persuading someone.

COMMON QUESTIONS ABOUT CIALDINI'S SIX TOOLS	
Will the tools always work and get someone to say yes?	No there are no guarantees. However, they increase the odds of a yes. There are many everyday examples of how people have used these to persuade.
Are there circumstances when the tools are very effective?	Yes, if there is a lot of uncertainty or complexity then people often fall back on these rules of thumb to make decisions. (Some unscrupulous people will deliberately cultivate uncertainty and complexity to make it more likely people will be persuaded by these tools)
Are they ethical?	The tools are neutral and can be used ethically or can be used unethically. Our advice is: do not use these methods to persuade someone to do something they do not want to do because it will bring short-term success, but long-term failure.

How Do The 6 Tools Work?

Like: people like people who are similar to them. People are more easily persuaded by people like them and so you should look for similarities between you and the person you are trying to persuade. There are many possible similarities. For example, where you went to school or college, your favourite sports, or favourite hobbies. Or, where you have worked or who you have worked with.

Reciprocity: People feel obliged to repay gifts and favours. When introduced to this tool, some people feel uncomfortable with the idea of giving gifts. While many organisations and individuals may not approve of gifts, they are proven persuaders. So rather than giving gifts unconnected with business, we suggest gifts of information are more appropriate. For example, if you are trying to influence a strategic customer then supplying them with a research article on their industry is appropriate. Or, if you discover an article in a newspaper or magazine, that is useful and relevant to them, forwarding this article to them is an appropriate business gift.

An interesting application of the reciprocity principle is often used by children with their parents. If you ask somebody for something and they say no to you, they are more likely to say yes to a subsequent request. In simple terms this is because they feel that they have asked you for a gift and you have not given the gift. So, shrewd children will ask their parents for one or two things which they know that their parents will say no to. This increases the chances of the parents saying yes to the next thing they ask for—the thing they really want.

This tactic is used by experienced negotiators, who repeatedly ask for something which the other party cannot give. This puts pressure on the other party to concede on something else. (In negotiating books, this is sometimes called a straw man—an artificial negotiating issue the other party cannot deliver.)

Telephone salespeople often use this tactic. They will call and say you have won a free night's accommodation (or a similar gift), all you have to do to collect your free gift is attend a seminar on the subject X. Using this tactic they will get far more people to attend the seminar.

Social Proof: this is probably the best understood of the six tools. People will follow the behaviour of other similar people to them. This can be other similar individuals or other similar organisations. So for example if you are trying to persuade a customer to use your services, mention the names of similar organisations or similar individuals who have used your services.

Apart from a positive use in business, this tool has an unfortunate use in frauds. In 2009, a Director of the Securities Division in Arizona suggested most fraud cases involve religious organisation and their constituents, or are directed at these organisations. So, the con men can use the tool in organisations where people view themselves as being very similar to each other, holding strong beliefs.

Consistency: in contrast to social proof this is probably the least understood of the six tools. Also, it is an insidious tool. It is an insidious tool because people align their behaviour with small commitments. The small commitments can seem insignificant and can be made many weeks or even months before the persuader asks for a bigger commitment.

An example is when another party asks for a small amount of your time to discuss an issue. The first meeting may be a brief telephone discussion. Once you have committed that small amount of time, then you are more likely to commit a similar or larger amount of time subsequently.

This is a very powerful tool that is very difficult to combat because the commitment asked for is often tiny and seems insignificant because you are not aware of the power of small commitments. Also, you are unaware of how this small commitment connects to a much bigger request that will be made days, weeks or even months later.

In business, when trying to persuade a senior manager if you can connect your proposal with some opinions they expressed in a meeting or issued in a document and show how your proposal is consistent with their words, this is very persuasive.

Authority: people defer to experts. In short the thinking is if an expert says I should do this then I probably should. The expert may be someone in medicine, wearing a white coat, or someone with all kinds of awards and diplomas on their office wall, or someone in a senior position.

In business, this is probably underused because people assume their expertise is self-evident. Also partly because many people are uncomfortable telling people about their achievements or qualifications. A technique we recommend to our clients is to get somebody else to introduce you and for that person to talk about your qualifications and experience. Having someone else introduce you in this way increases your credibility substantially and makes you far more persuasive.

A less effective alternative is to send a biography in advance or to put the information on your website. This is less effective because the information has more impact when it is delivered by somebody else and delivered by somebody else in person.

Scarcity: this is a popular tool used by many. For example TV advertisers promise the first 200 callers will get special gift, or retailers brag about special offers for a limited time and with a limited stock. Whenever you hear there is a limited stock or limited time, then be aware the tool of scarcity may be being used on you.

In business, this tool can be used by explaining how you are providing this particular customer with exclusive access to this information, or that the information or your experience is rare, or providing some unique benefits. The driving force of this tool is a strong human instinct to avoid making a loss on missing out on something.

Now that you understand the six tools, we provide a form we find useful as a prompt when we are creating persuasive messages. The form lists the six tools of persuasion, along with some useful questions to prompt ideas for how you could use the tools in a particular persuasive message.

CREATING A PERSUASIVE MESSAGE USING THE SIX TOOLS

Tool	Useful Questions
Like People like people who are like them. Look for similarities.	Where do they come from? What do they do in their spare time? Do you have any acquaintances in common? Do you have any experiences or problems in common?
Reciprocity People feel obliged to repay gifts and favours.	Can you give them some information? Can you give them a lead? Can you entertain them with food or at a sports occasion? Can you ask for something that you know they cannot give you?
Social Proof People follow the lead of other similar people. Use peer power when you can.	Can you point to lots of other similar people or companies who use your services?
Consistency People align their behaviour with small commitments. Make their commitments active, public and voluntary.	Can you get people to agree to a small trial? Can you get people to attend a brief meeting? Can you get people to commit to a position publicly? Can you get people to provide a testimonial about your services? Can you get people to visit your facilities?
Authority People defer to experts. Expose your expertise; do not assume it is self-evident.	Can you show any independent experts opinions of your services? Can you show qualifications, certification or accreditation? Can you show the opinion of a reputable (high-profile) customer? Can you show them newspaper or magazine articles?
Scarcity People want more of what they can have less of. Highlight unique benefits and exclusive information.	Can you suggest limited availability? Can you suggest limited time for an offer? Can you suggest you have secret, proprietary or rare information?

Colossal Sports case

For the Colossal Sports case, to persuade the managers Louise might use the tool like the table below.

CREATING A PERSUASIVE MESSAGE USING THE SIX TOOLS: COLOSSAL SPORTS	
Tool	**How could you apply these to persuade the managers?**
Like People like people who are like them. Look for similarities.	Find examples of other similar sports companies who have adopted new information systems and produced better results. Connect with the managers by reminding them of the challenges and changes Louise has experienced with them. Acknowledge their emotions. Summarise the emotions you think some of the managers may be feeling. Suggest you have had similar feelings, but understanding the proposed system has alleviated some of those feelings. Try to find similarities between some of the people who will implement the systems and the managers: "Like you John, the systems analyst comes from New Zealand"; "Jenny, you might be interested to know the program manager raves about our products and is always eating them in our meetings."; "Simon, you won't believe who manages their customer centre, the former Australian captain Alan Border."
Reciprocity People feel obliged to repay gifts and favours.	During Louise's interviews, each of the managers—John, Simon and Jennifer—mentioned specific business issues that were causing them big problems. Speak with the managing partner of our auditors, ask if he has any research papers or reports that might help on those issues, then get them and give them to the relevant manager. Try to find books that might help deal with the issues and buy a copy for them.
Social Proof People follow the lead of other similar people. Use peer power when you can.	Ask the IT company for the names and numbers of managers in similar companies selling equipment, apparel or food. Call them and ask for their opinion of the system, the benefits. Also, ask what they would do differently if they installed the system again. Create a slide quoting some of their words.

Consistency People align their behaviour with small commitments. Make their commitments active, public and voluntary.	Before the presentation, interview the managers individually, ask them what they want out of the system and what they don't want. Tailor you presentations to show how you meet their needs. Then at the beginning of the presentation, summarise what they told you and ask them if that's correct. Then through the presentation connect back to their comments, for example "So John, that gives you the daily report you said was critical; and Simon, that eliminates 5 days of work for your people; and Jennifer, that gives you the flexibility you need."
Authority People defer to experts. Expose your expertise; do not assume it is self-evident.	Bring copies of the independent report written by IBM that shows this system is the best for businesses like ours with independent divisions. Mention the postgraduate course in information systems you took after qualifying as an accountant.
Scarcity People want more of what they can have less of. Highlight unique benefits and exclusive information.	Highlight that, unlike the existing system, the new system allows them to access financial reports on their iPhones and their iPads. So, when out of the office anywhere in the world, they can quickly answer questions from customers or the CEO without having to wait for the Sydney office to open. Highlight that the IT firm already works with the largest sports firms in China and India who use the system and are happy to arrange site visits. These site visits would provide useful market intelligence and contacts that may lead to opportunities for faster growth.

These 6 tools are very powerful. Our advice is: do not use these tools to persuade someone to do something they do not want to do because using them unethically will bring short-term success, but long-term failure.

Using these tools ethically to help you craft persuasive messages will make you a much more powerful persuader and bring you long-term success.

Section 2
Prepare to Persuade

Success occurs when
opportunity meets preparation

Insight 6
Plan Your Preparation

"Extinction, of course, is irreversible. And even heroic measures to keep an endangered species going don't stand much of a chance without profound changes in human behaviour and genuine protection of the species' habitat."

David Suzuki

Planning to persuade is like planning any other project. It means setting clear goals and allowing yourself one important commodity—time. Even the most experienced presenter should not leave organising a presentation to the last minute. To deliver a persuasive presentation every time, you will need to be comfortable with the subject matter of the presentation, but you will also need to manage logistics, such as choosing a venue, making handouts and preparing visuals. That is why it is crucial to create a plan before you even start your research. Some simple project management skills will prove invaluable.

Planning your Persuasion

To begin preparing your presentation, start with six questions—why, who, what, how, where and when.

Why	Why have you been asked to speak?
	Why specifically you?
Who	Who is in your audience?
	Who else will be presenting?

What	What is your main message?
	What is your objective?
	What action do you want the audience to take?
	What is the scope of your presentation?
	What facilities are available?
How	How should you deliver your message?
	How long are you speaking for?
	How much detail should you include?
	How do you get to the location?
Where	Where will you be speaking?
When	When is the presentation?
	When will you test the facilities?

It would be difficult to list every task that might be necessary when preparing a presentation, because every presentation is different. However, the list above will help you begin thinking about your presentation time. Then have a brief look at the Contents Summary to get an idea of each task you need to plan. To help you prepare, the following paragraphs provide an outline of the presentation planning process.

The first step in the presentation process is to determine your objective. Why are you giving the presentation? What are you hoping your audience will take from the presentation? What do you hope to achieve? How do you want the audience to react? What do you want the audience to do next? Answer these questions, then summarise in one sentence what you are trying to say and what you want the audience to do.

Next, brainstorm your initial ideas. Organise these preliminary thoughts into between three and seven main points and arrange the points in a logical order. These will form the skeleton of your presentation. Each point must be researched thoroughly so you can provide supporting evidence for your ideas.

After the initial research, you can begin to draft your presentation and visualise your ideas and data. Concentrate on your main insights and decide which photographs, charts and graphs will complement your presentation. Other parts of this book will guide you through all of these aspects, but for the initial planning stage, you will need to have an idea of the tasks and plot these on a time line. This is what project management is all about—planning each task to achieve a goal. So, think about what you need to do, write this down, and arrange a sequence of events.

Create a time line

Many presenters have attempted to estimate the hours of preparation that go into each minute of a presentation. However, there is no way of knowing exactly how many hours you will need to prepare your presentation. Each situation is different and it will depend on your experience, your existing knowledge of the topic and many other factors. We suggest you divide your presentation into smaller tasks and mark these on a time line. This will help you to estimate how long you think each stage will take.

Work with the goal in mind—the day of the presentation. With the help of the Tool Kit, list every aspect involved in preparing for this presentation and devise a realistic time line, with a list of tasks that should be achieved by a certain date.

Below is an example of a simple plan for a presentation.

OBJECTIVE	TASKS	DATE
Arrange the logistics	Liaise with the organiser to determine the venue, audience size, breaks, seating arrangement, length of presentation, etc. Book flights and accommodation.	1–4 July
Understand Audience	Read publications and website of the company/companies you are presenting to. Interview random sample of staff members.	1–5 July
Research Data	Read general books on the subject. Read journal articles. Interview an expert. Cull material to main points.	1–8 July
Write Close	Write the close.	9–10 July
Write Opening	Write the opening.	9–10 July
Structure Contents	Write content or substance using a model.	11 July
Questions	Anticipate questions.	11 July
Follow up	Plan a follow up.	11 July
Visuals	Decide on best visual medium. Prepare visuals.	11–12 July
Handouts	Prepare handouts.	13 July

Next we see a plan produced by Louise at Colossal Sports.

PLANNING TOOL: COLOSSAL SPORTS

Presentation Topic	Promotion of a new information system for our company, Colossal Sports.
Date	3 October.
Time	10.00am–2.30am (with 2 × 10 min breaks, 1 × 30 min break). Duration: 4.5 hours including breaks.
Location	Executive Board Room (London office).
Coordinator and contact number	Linda: extension 456.
What prompted the request for your presentation?	The Directors want 15% growth in company profits year-on-year for the next five years. The Directors want specific information on the costs and profits across the company, to help improve profitability. The new system will require support from the heads of each department. I need to persuade the heads we should change from recording costs and profits for only the company to recording costs and profits by division. I also need to convince them this system is the best one for keeping records of their costs and profits.
Number of Attendees	3.
Who is your audience?	The heads of each division—Equipment (John), Apparel (Simon), Food (Jennifer).
Who will be presenting before and after you?	Nobody.
Will the context be formal or informal?	Formal (business).
What are the goals of the presentation?	To persuade the audience of the merits of the new information system. By the end of the presentation, I want them to adopt the idea, approve in principle the proposal for $4 million capital and give their personal and active commitment to implementing the new system.

PLANNING TOOL: COLOSSAL SPORTS

What are your main points?	The Directors want 15% growth of profits year-on-year for the next five years and are very angry at the loss of the Marbella account.
	Recording profits by department will help them understand and increase the performance (profit) of each department. It will allow tracking of costs and trends and help in predicting future profits.
	This system is best for Colossal Sports because it combines the best of the systems used in the industry and will be tailored to meet our specific needs.
	While this system is more expensive than other systems on the market, it will be better for long term growth and has the flexibility for managers to produce their own special reports fast.
What facilities will you have access to?	Laptop computer, projector, whiteboard.
What organisation will be required (flights, accommodation, catering, etc)?	Flights and accommodation booked by PA.
	Refreshments on arrival: Tea, coffee and water.
	Morning tea to arrive at 11.30am—cakes and fresh drinks.
	Lunch to arrive at 1.00pm—sandwiches and fruit juice.
	Organiser: Pam Jones, Administrative Officer (ext 324).
Outline your timeline	I have three weeks to prepare this presentation.
	My to-do list:
	Week 1:
	Research the data:
	• Familiarise myself with the new system. Play with the data and become confident in using the program.
	• Create sample data to demonstrate the program.
	• Look at other companies that use similar systems to see how it has helped them.
	Research the audience:
	Brainstorm the advantages and disadvantages the program will have for each department. Pre-empt objections. Examine the figures for each department to see what weaknesses might be exposed in each department.
	Week 2: Closing stage, Opening stage, and Content stage.
	Week 3: Create visuals and handouts. Practice and refine the presentation.

And similarly, a plan for the Community Garden Proposal

PLANNING TOOL: COMMUNITY GARDEN	
Presentation Topic	Why the community needs a sustainable garden?
Date	11th April
Time	11:00
Location	Council Chambers
Coordinator and contact number	Ms Hannah Armstrong 02 9498 4563
What prompted the request for your presentation?	In response to a community desire, I set up the meeting with Winona.
Number of Attendees	6
Who is your audience?	Council Members: Mr. John Woods from the Planning Committee Ms. Susan Watson from the Sustainability Reference Committee Miss Clementine Silvestre from the Community Reference Committee Mr. Elliott Smith from the Heritage Reference Committee Mr. Hamish Hogan from the Open Space Reference Committee Miss Danielle Stephens from the Ku-ring-gai Traffic Committee
Who will be presenting before and after you?	Nobody
Will the context be formal or informal?	Formal
What are the goals of the presentation?	To gain council approval and support to go ahead with the community garden

PLANNING TOOL: COMMUNITY GARDEN

What are your main points?	The Community wants the garden (provide evidence of those in favour of the garden) Benefits of the garden: • promote community spirit • council will be seen as one that listens to the community • increased popularity of the council in the up-coming election • promote a healthy and happy community lifestyle What is involved: • costs • provision of a plot of land • labour • maintenance
What facilities will you have access to?	Council Chambers Boardroom AV system and laptop
What organisation will be required (flights, accommodation, catering, etc)?	Booking of the boardroom—confirm with Winona 1 week prior Prepare the platter of organic food for the councillors to taste, grown in a neighbouring community garden
Outline your timeline	I have 4 weeks to prepare the presentation. Week 1—Research other community gardens: • Explore other community gardens in Sydney and speak to those involved in dealing with their Council to create it • Take photos of thriving community gardens • Research the costs of setting up a garden Week 2—Research the audience: • Find common desire of the council and the community to show the council why they should want the garden too • Find supporting council legislation to encourage them to agree to the garden Week 3—Prepare Presentation • Prepare handouts and visuals • Have all material scrutinised and edited by a friend Week 4—Practice presentation and gather food samples for the platter

Insight 7
The Presentation Preparation Process

*"I believe my choices today can shape
what happens tomorrow."*

Anon

The Presentation Preparation Process

This Insight gives an overview of the process of preparing a presentation. However, before we go any further, we must provide a mental health warning.

First, this Insight looks at the critical elements of a presentation, not at every detail. Greater detail is available in later Insights.

Second, to some people, the order of the stages may seem counter-intuitive, or even a little bit Irish. But while people often laugh at the stereotypically unique way that Irish people give instructions and directions, counter-intuitive insight can often be helpful. (By the way, one of the authors has an Irish background. If you ever meet them both at the same time, you will not have too much trouble working out which one it is!)

The Five Stages of the Process

Understand Audience	Research Data	Write Close	Write Opening	Structure Content

Understand Audience. The first step in the presentation process is to understand your audience. Who are they? What are their attitudes, aspirations and beliefs? What do you want the audience to do next? Answer these questions, then summarise your message and the response you want from the audience in one sentence.

Research Data. Next, research your subject. After this research, brainstorm your initial ideas. Organise these preliminary thoughts into three to seven main points. These main points will form the skeleton of your presentation. Each point needs to be researched thoroughly so you can provide supporting evidence for your ideas.

Write Close. In our seminars, the timing of this stage often raises some eyebrows and hands. People ask two questions—"Why is this stage here?" and "How can I write the close now?"

The 'why' question is simple to answer. First, it is faster and more effective to prepare the presentation when you write the close first, as suggested by David Peoples, who wrote *Presentations Plus*. Writing the close first helps focus your attention on the outcome you want from the presentation. When you move on to the content stage, it is faster because you will be more ruthless about choosing powerful content because you will have a clear picture what you want the audience to do next.

The second reason to write the close first is because the close will have a significant impact on the audience's impression of the presenter. If you write the close at the end of your preparation, you may not have time to do it well.

The question, "How can I write the close now?" is simple to answer. First, look at your audience analysis and understand what you want the audience to do. Second, look at your one sentence summary. Third, look at your research and summarise the evidence you have collected. Collect all of these together, and write the close. For example, "based on the five pieces of evidence, we have seen that … and I now ask you to …"

At this stage, the close does not have to be word-perfect. However, the close must clearly show how the evidence leads to the action you want the audience to take. The clearer your thinking, the better the close, which is key to Persuading for Results.

Write Opening. The opening is a critical time, similar to the close. It determines the audience's initial impression of the presenter. In the opening, you must capture the attention of the audience and connect with their interests. Most of the information necessary is available from a previous stage 'understanding the audience'. In essence, you must answer one question for the audience, "Why should I listen to you?"

Structure Your Content. Your presentation should be structured carefully. This does not necessarily mean dazzling your audience with dozens of headings and subheadings. It just means letting them know where the presentation is heading, so they can prepare themselves for the journey. Some of the most effective presenters appear very relaxed and natural, but actually have a very clear structure. Their skill is in making the structure flow in a way that looks effortless.

During the planning stage, think about what you want the audience to remember from the presentation. Psychologists tell us that most people can remember between three and seven things in their short-term memory. This obviously varies with interest, attention, intelligence and fatigue.

Some presenters rely on the theory of sevens. That is, the idea that an audience cannot easily remember more than seven ideas. Joyce Kupsh, in her book *Create High Impact Business Reports*, illustrates how much people prefer seven with a list of things associated with seven including:

Things	Days of the week
	Colours of the spectrum
Movies	The Seven Dwarfs
	The Seven Voyages of Sinbad
	The magnificent Seven
Geography	Seas
	Continents
	Wonders of the World
	Hills of Rome

While some presenters recommend seven, others suggest as few as three. McKinsey & Co is one of the top management consultancies in the world. McKinsey provides insight into some of the most complex business problems and employs some of the smartest consultants. According to Ethan Rasiel, their advice is to aim for three main points. Never more than five but three is best.

What do we recommend? Well, three is ideal for complex material because it will make the presentation clearer and easier to remember. We suggest using three main points when the presentation is critical and the content is complex.

Four main points can sometimes be elegantly presented in the form of a 2 by 2 square or matrix (a square divided into quarters). This is a very popular format because most audiences can remember four points and the matrix is easy to understand and remember.

As with many business issues there is a trade-off. For some presentations the audience will not need the simplicity or there will not be enough time or resources to prepare a simple presentation. If necessary, use up to seven main points, but never more. Remember, the more points, the greater the risk that your message will be misunderstood or forgotten. If in doubt, aim for fewer ideas.

NUMBER OF MAIN IDEAS	COMMENTS
3	Will make complex information simpler. Takes significant time and effort. Aids persuasion.
4	Often can be represented in a box with quarters (a 2 by 2 matrix or box). A 2 by 2 box is an efficient way of presenting information and helps make the message more memorable.
5	Recommended for most presentations as a trade-off between clarity, time and resources.
7	Maximum to allow people to remember the structure. The audience may not act because they do not remember or understand. This is the fastest to create.

That completes the overview of the planning process. With the framework in place, it is time to examine the details in the following Insights.

Insight 8
Understand Your Audience

"Seek first to understand, then to be understood!"

St. Francis

| Understand Audience | Research Data | Write Close | Write Opening | Structure Content |

Who are they?

One of the foundations for your persuasion is, knowing who is in your audience, what they expect and how they will judge you. When Persuading For Results, this applies whether you are making an informal presentation to a small group or a formal presentation to a large audience.

If you are in the enviable position of having control over the invitation list, think carefully about audience size and structure. Should you invite just the decision makers and power brokers, or a cross-section of the company? Does the venue impose space constraints? What size audience would be ideal for this particular presentation?

To persuade an audience effectively, you need to understand their knowledge-base and motives for attending. Have they chosen to, or been asked to, attend? What do they know about the topic? Who are the decision-makers? Which individuals have the power to put your recommendations into action? Who is likely to oppose your message?

At this point some people will be saying, "I don't have time to research the audience because I am too busy building the presentation." However, without a thorough understanding of the audience, the presenter will not be able to appeal to their self-interest and all the time spent building content will be in vain.

Think back to the Bayer case study. To sell to farmers, a distributor needs to understand the science of Zapp and how it is practically applied to sheep. This knowledge of the distributors' needs, led to the design of a product launch which incorporated a hands-on demonstration that bowled the distributors over.

The effort you put into researching the audience should correlate with the importance of the presentation. Sometimes you may wish to consider behaviour with a tool like DiSC®. DiSC® classifies behaviour into four styles and each style prefers a different communications style. We find DiSC® easy to learn and powerful to use. Some people prefer to use Myers-Briggs or MBTI, however we find the 16 styles are too complex to be practical in most situations. The work of Paul Tieger using temperaments is a simplification and an improvement. (See *Insight 11—Tailor to your target* for more information)

In practice, it is likely the audience will consist of people with a mixture of preferences. This means tailoring your message to all types, but emphasising the styles preferred by the influential people. We discuss this further in *Insight 11—Tailor to your target*. For now, let's look at how to understand your audience.

Explore Their Background

Knowing about your audience will largely determine the content and delivery style of your presentation. Discover as much demographical information as you can. Ask questions about:

- Average age.
- Occupations.
- Gender.
- Educational background.
- Cultural and political beliefs.
- Professional backgrounds.

Ask the organiser for a list of the audience members several weeks before the presentation. If possible, make sure the list includes information about the positions and organisations of your audience members. For added impact with a small group, memorise the names of the audience. If the group is too large for this, at least make sure you memorise the names of key people, and can pronounce unfamiliar names.

Research the Company or Industry

To find out about your audience, read up on their industry and find out about the business. You will be amazed by what you can glean just by reading annual reports, websites and prospectuses. Many industries also have a representative body that you can contact to learn about current issues, challenges or opportunities in the industry.

What is Their Existing Knowledge?

It is important to have a general idea of what the audience already knows about the topic. You can adapt the delivery of your presentation as you go with a simple "hands up if you are familiar with these facts and figures". However, it helps if you know ahead of time.

If the audience is well informed on the subject, the content of your presentation should be pitched at their level. Focusing too much on the basics, risks 'switching off' the audience. Conversely, an uninformed audience will require more instruction and less depth so the presentation does not 'go over their heads'.

Audience Size

The audience size will have an impact on your presentation. Gaining this information before the presentation will help you plan the delivery technique. Delivering to large groups relies more heavily on a one-way style of communication, whereas with a smaller group you can allow more interaction.

So, smaller groups are often easier to Persuade for Results, because a persuasive presenter can interact with the audience more effectively and tailor the presentation as they go. Interactive presentations are also possible with a larger audience—it is just more challenging.

Analysing the audience

For small groups we identify individuals, but for larger groups we identify groups of employees by department, function or stage of the business process. Once we identify the groups or individuals then we can use many tools. In this case we will use the Colossal Sports case study to illustrate a powerful tool—the Attitude-Influence chart from Grundy and Brown.

In the Attitude-Influence diagram, we first analyse the attitude and influence of the individuals or groups and then plot these on a chart. In essence, the chart shows that we need to be concerned most about the people with high influence. However, be warned that some people or groups with high influence are not obvious from an organisation chart.

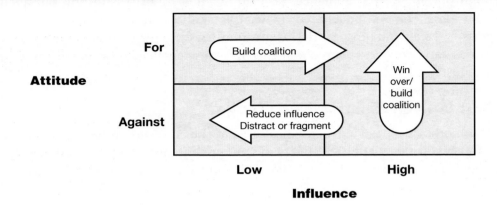

Worry about stakeholders who have more influence

For

Build coalition

Win over/ build coalition

Attitude

Against

Reduce influence Distract or fragment

Low   High

Influence

	ATTITUDE			INFLUENCE		
	Against	Neutral	For	Low	Neutral	High
Simon (Apparel)			●	●		
John (Equipment)	●					●
Jennifer (Food)		●				●

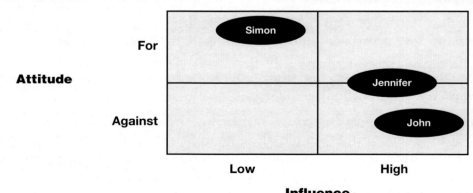

Worry about stakeholders who have more influence

For

Simon

Attitude

Jennifer

Against

John

Low   High

Influence

In this example we can see that we need to try to build a coalition with John, or if this does not work then either reduce his influence or distract him. Also we need to build a coalition with Simon and Jennifer.

AUDIENCE RESEARCH TOOL: COLOSSAL SPORTS	
Who is in your audience? Who are the key members?	The heads of each department — Equipment (John), Apparel (Simon), Food (Jennifer).
What is their motivation for attending?	They are obliged to attend. However they are motivated by the potential this has to affect their department. I have briefed them (via email) of the date and reason for the presentation.
How are they related to your topic?	They are integral to implementing this system. They will be responsible for putting into practice and overseeing the success of the new system. If they do not believe in the benefits of the new system, the project will fail. Also, the implementation will affect their profit because it will cost them for the time their people are in training, plus the cost of the software over the next five years.
What do they know about you? What do they need to know?	The audience is familiar with me. I have liaised with them on many issues over the years. At the end of each financial year, I present the results to them and the targets for the forthcoming year.
What is their current knowledge of the topic?	They know nothing about the new system. They are familiar with budgeting and analysing profits and costs.
What do they want/ need to know?	They need to know the concerns of the Board, specifically, the anger of the board at the loss of Marbella and that the board is determined to achieve 15% growth in profits year-on-year for the next five years. They need to know about the new system and how it will effect their department. They will want to know that it will not be detrimental to their team, but will lift their performance. They will want to know why this system out-performs other cheaper systems.
What is the audience's attitude to you and your topic?	Their attitude towards me will be fairly tough. As I am involved with the numbers at Colossal Sports, they will see me as a technical person, who does not understand the people side of the business. The topic is relevant to them but they will feel some resistance to change and will be worried about their numbers being monitored and analysed more closely than before.

How do you expect the audience to react to your presentation?	I expect they will feel threatened at the prospect of being scrutinised. Simon will be most receptive to the idea, as the new system will finally show just how much his marketing team builds the profits of the other departments. His 35% profit is a modest indication of the true profits he generates for the company.
	John has a reputation for resisting change and will be particularly against this idea, as his team is already busy making a great profit. He will see little advantage in changing the way he is doing things.
	Jennifer is fairly new to Colossal Sports and as a newly appointed manager she is full of energy and fresh ideas. Jennifer is currently running at a loss, but her high growth figures are promising. She will be concerned that the detailed analysis of her costs will prevent her continuing with her rapid growth. She wants to maintain the freedom and flexibility to take a different approach to the other divisions.
	All three managers will be reluctant to commit to the initial cost of implementing the system, as well as the ongoing cost of maintaining the system.
What techniques would be best for this audience?	It is important to emphasise the urgency of the situation. I will also outline the concerns of the Board and shareholders.
	For John's sake, I will take the approach that it is not a 'change' but a small modification to the way things are currently done. I will incorporate good quotes because John is influenced by historical figures.
	E.g. "The best time to repair the roof is while the sun is shining." John F Kennedy.
	I will show John that his daily routine will not be greatly different and he will get some advantages out of the system—he will be able to manage his costs better to get more profit. Having been a long-standing member of the Colossal Sports team, his opinion will influence Simon and Jennifer.
What techniques would be best for this audience? **(Jennifer)**	Jennifer has a good business head and will take on the new system if she thinks it is a good investment for the long-term growth of her department. To convince Jennifer, I will use graphs, charts and data.
	Also, fast-growing divisions need different measures to mature divisions. In fast-growing divisions, annual budgets can quickly be irrelevant. For example, if you budget $200,000 for operating expenses based on a sales target of $2 million, then you are unlikely to care if the expenses are $300,000, if the sales are actually $4 million? A better measure for fast-growing divisions is to look at expenses as a percentage of sales. The new system produces reports in this format. This will be useful to Jennifer and help her manage her business and negotiate with the CEO for more resources.

What techniques would be best for this audience? **(Simon)**	To convince Simon, I will show how the new system measures more than just purchasing costs and will quantify how much each department costs other departments. This is one feature of the new system that other systems on the market simply cannot match.
What are the demographics of the audience? (Age, occupation, religion, socioeconomic status, gender, education, political background, etc).	All three audience members are divisional managers, with first degrees or higher. Simon is 35, John is 53 and Jennifer is 29. They are smart and experienced business people, with no known prejudices.
What are your research findings relating to the industry/company background?	Colossal Sports has a reputation amongst athletes and the general public alike as being a reliable and customer friendly franchise. Financial figures over the past ten years show increasing profit up until the past three years, when profits began dropping. While Colossal Sports profits are dropping, profits for our major competitor—Sports House—jumped 30% last year.
How will you follow up your presentation?	Email each audience member—thank for attendance, attach journal article relating to the benefits of the new system. Let them know I will call on Monday to touch base and organise a meeting to consider the details of implementing the system.

AUDIENCE RESEARCH TOOL: COMMUNITY GARDEN

Who is in your audience? Who are the key members?	Mr. John Woods from the Planning Committee Ms. Susan Watson from the Sustainability Committee-Key Member Miss Clementine Silvestre from the Community Committee-Key Member Mr. Elliott Smith from the Heritage Committee Mr. Hamish Hogan from the Open Space Committee Miss Danielle Stephens from the Ku-ring-gai Traffic Committee
What is their motivation for attending?	An interest in promoting sustainability. Also, Mr. John Woods wishes to boost his popularity as there is an upcoming election.

How are they related to your topic?	All members must approve the project for the garden to receive the allocated plot and funding.
What do they know about you? What do they need to know?	Previous e-mail outlining my qualifications, which include a Permaculture Design Course, living in the area for many years and my involvement with the community.
What is their current knowledge of the topic?	Knowledge of a previous community garden in a nearby suburb.
What do they want/ need to know?	Why there is a need for a community garden. How much it will approximately cost. Possible plot sites. The benefits of a community garden. Access to the design proposal. Aims and objectives. Plans and Management options. Health and Safety Systems. Social and organisational systems.
What is the audience's attitude to you and your topic?	Mixed.
How do you expect the audience to react to your presentation?	Positive response: • Ms. Susan Watson from the Sustainability Committee • Miss Clementine Silvestre from the Community Committee • Mr. John Woods from the Planning Committee • Mr. Elliott Smith from the Heritage Committee Neutral response: • Miss Danielle Stephens from the Ku-ring-gai Traffic Committee Negative response: • Mr. Hamish Hogan from the Open Space Committee
What techniques would be best for this audience? **Positive**	Provide fruit at the beginning of the meeting. Use feel-good pictures and examples. Reinforce that you share the same values for the community as the council does. Show that you are organised and that you plan to make the garden self-sustainable and community run.

What techniques would be best for this audience? Neutral	Emphasise the maximum benefits for minimal costs.
	Emphasis on community support.
	Show the importance and benefits the garden will have to the community and how it will fulfil sustainability and waste management commitments.
	Lend them some literature on community gardens, and possibly even arrange a tour of a nearby established community garden.
What techniques would be best for this audience? Negative	Address all of their objections and show that the benefits outweigh the negatives.
	Address cost issues and public liability concerns by outlining community funding and insurance plans.
	Allow time for questions and be prepared with answers.
	Frame it as minimising losses and gaining a community recreational centre for minimal cost or effort from the council.
How will you follow up your presentation?	Offer for them to visit an established community garden if they want to see it in action before deciding.
	Arrange for a follow up meeting to hear the answer to the proposal.

Understanding Individuals with the Internet

When persuading for results, you can use the Internet to understand the individuals you are persuading. The simplest way is to search using Google, simply type in the name of the individual. So for example using www.google.com.au, if you were to search for Stephen Kozicki you would find plenty of hits, 18,100 results. As we explain in Insight 14, putting the search text in quotation marks reduces the number of hits, so searching for "Stephen Kozicki" returns 6,370 results.

When looking at the results of a Google search, look at their professional activities and professional interests. Also look at any references to social activities. It is surprising how much information you can find from Google, however there are other sources of information on the Internet.

One of the most useful sources for business is LinkedIn (www.linkedin.com). So, if you start with Google and for example search for: "Stephen Kozicki" LinkedIn, (if the person has a LinkedIn profile) then you will find a link to the person's LinkedIn profile. In the profile are details of education and work experience, so it is a rich source of information. To access the full profile, you must be connected to the person, but there is some information available on public profiles. LinkedIn offers many ways of searching for people including by name, by company and by geography.

One of the most useful features of LinkedIn is connections—who people are connected to. If you have a LinkedIn profile and search for somebody, then you will see if you already know anyone who knows your persuasion target. If someone is already in your network is connected to persuasion target, then you could contact them and ask for background information on the individual. Also, if appropriate, you could ask them to introduce you to your persuasion target. Being introduced to your persuasion target by someone who already knows them increases your credibility.

Even if you do not already know anybody who knows the persuasion target, try searching in LinkedIn for the company's name. Again you may be surprised to find that you already know somebody who works in the target company. Again, you could contact this person and ask for background information on the persuasion.

With the increase in social networking sites, we expect you will be able to find more information about your persuasion targets, when you start with a simple Google search.

Insight 9
Buying styles

"Business today consists in persuading crowds."
T. S. Eliot

Understand Audience	Research Data	Write Close	Write Opening	Structure Content

Influencing organisations — Influence people differently

When influencing organisations to buy something—a product, a service or an idea—organisations can look complex and overwhelming. There are many different titles in organisations and despite the organisations' official processes, many people influence the process of buying a product or buying a service—or simply buying an idea.

Many books recommend identifying the decision maker and going directly to them; read on to discover why this is a major mistake.

While organisations can look complex and overwhelming, despite the many different titles, with over 30 years experience we can define five buying styles:

1. Decision-makers
2. Influencers
3. Recommenders
4. Gatekeepers
5. End users

How to identify a buying style

The table below summarises how to identify each buying style

BUYING STYLE	CHARACTERISTICS
Decision Makers	Authority to give final approval on decision (or project, or idea)
	Can start a purchasing process in the organisation, or can start change in an organisation
	Focuses on strategic issues (e.g. customers and competitors) and the impact on the whole of the business
	Focuses on results, ROI, cash, profits
Influencers	Often influences final decision
	Usually in close relationship with the decision maker
	Have personal/position power within the organisation
	Sometimes active opinion leaders in the industry
Recommenders	Able to recommend the purchase to decision maker
	Uses specifications and standards to judge
	Persuasive ability with decision makers due to their technical expertise
	Examples: purchasing, accounting, engineering, and legal, Head of Pharmacy in hospitals
Gatekeepers	Sceptical of any project, information, idea/concept, new process or product that challenges the way they currently do business
	Every item, data, dollar is scrutinised
	Can be disruptive
	Only approach when well prepared and you can answer their questions with data or evidence
End Users	Uses product or service
	May have input on buying process based on performance
	Important link in buying process
	Key end users should be a critical part of your persuasion strategy

To show how to identify a buying style, we will apply them to two different cases. First, influencing an engineering organisation to buy new drawing software and second, influencing a hospital to buy a new drug.

Influencing an engineering organisation to buy new drawing software

Decision-maker: The decision-maker is the managing director. For a large purchase like this, they must approve the purchase. However, choosing new drawing software is a complex decision because it has a major effect on the productivity and operating costs of the organisation.

The advice of many other books is to deal only with the decision-makers. As you'll see, this is wrong.

Influencers: one of the obvious influencers is the IT manager. They must ensure software is compatible with existing hardware and ensure they have the skills to operate the software. In addition, they will need to examine service and maintenance costs to ensure the costs fit their operating budgets.

A less obvious influencer is the factory manager, who uses the information provided by engineering and may import some data into manufacturing systems. Their interests are typically data formats and also whether the new software will reduce the time taken in engineering.

Recommenders: The two main recommenders will be the engineering director and the purchasing manager. The engineering director will be interested in how the software affects the productivity of his department. The purchasing manager will be interested in the purchase price, commercial terms and ongoing service and maintenance costs.

Gatekeepers: One gatekeeper is the accountant, who will scrutinise the business case carefully. Another gatekeeper is the lawyer or company secretary who will scrutinise the contract terms carefully.

End Users: The main end users are draughtsman and the software will have a major effect on their productivity. Any reduction in productivity will increase the time taken to produce designs and could increase the lead-time for their products. Another important factor for them is how quickly they can learn the new system.

Another group of end users are the service engineers who, when on customer sites, use the software to read drawings on their laptops. The service engineers need software which allows them to open drawings quickly and does not slow down the other software on their laptops. Typically this is a small group that many may ignore. However, the service operations are often very profitable and so reducing the productivity of this group is likely to prevent the purchase of new software. In addition, this group are in contact with customers every day. So, software that reduces their productivity could reduce customer satisfaction. So, this small group can have a major influence on this decision. So, we see the advice from other books, to speak to only the decision maker, is simply wrong.

CASE STUDY 1: Influencing an engineering organisation to buy new drawing software	
Buying Style	**Some of The Different People Who Need to be Influenced**
Decision Makers	Managing Director
Influencers	IT Manager
	Factory Manager
Recommenders	Engineering Director
	Purchasing Manager
Gatekeepers	Accountant(Business Case)
	Lawyer(Contract terms)
End Users	Draughtsman
	Service engineers

Influencing a hospital to buy a new drug to prevent blood clotting

Changing a drug is a big decision for a hospital, with health and economic consequences.

Decision-maker: The decision-maker is the hospital manager. However, the hospital manager would not make a decision without consulting many other people. So, even if you could meet with the hospital manager, they would not make a decision based on you presenting them information. The advice of other books to only meet with the decision-makers is naive and misguided.

Influencers: In the hospital this is the most complex group. People's buying style depends on the kind of drug and their roles on committees. Typically, hospitals will have a drug evaluation committee or a drug and therapeutics committee. The committee evaluates the drug technically and economically compared to alternative treatments. In complex evaluations, committees consider many factors including drug costs, drug effects, length of hospital stay and hospital costs.

Obviously, committee members have direct influence on the decision. Also, for a drug to prevent clotting, other people will be influencers too. Heads of department who are specialists, staff specialists or visiting medical officers (haematology and vascular) will be influencers. Visiting medical officers are specialists who provide services to more than one hospital. This increases the complexity of persuasion because visiting medical officers are influenced and influence practices in more hospitals than the target hospital. In some hospitals, advanced trainees will also influence the decision.

From this brief description of influencers, it is obvious the advice of many books to only deal with the decision-makers is wrong. This wrong advice assumes that because the decision-makers are at the top of the organisation chart, they control the behaviour of experts. The hospital manager cannot ignore the opinions of influencers.

Recommenders: in the hospital the recommender is the chief pharmacist. As we have seen from the discussion of influencers, the chief pharmacist is not the only expert, who will influence the hospital manager.

Gatekeepers: Two gatekeepers are the procurement manager and a lawyer in the legal department. Their main influence is on contract terms. The procurement manager will also try to influence pricing and other commercial terms.

End-users: The end users are nurses. Some persuaders may be tempted to assume the end users will use the drugs they are given. However, nurses are normally union members and so if a drug makes their job harder, then there is potential for industrial relations problems.

In addition, typically 60% of hospital costs are staff costs. So, hospital managers are unlikely to approve drugs which reduced the productivity of nurses. Therefore it is critical for the persuader to meet with the nurses and understand how a new drug will affect their productivity. Given the importance of nurse productivity, showing how the new drug will increase nurses' productivity will be very persuasive to the hospital manager.

Again end users can have a major influence on this decision. So, we see the advice to only speak to the decision maker is simply wrong. Therefore, to persuade for results we must influence the users as well as the decision-makers.

CASE STUDY 2: Influencing a hospital to buy a new drug to prevent blood clotting	
Buying Style	**Some of The Different people who need to be influenced**
Decision Makers	Hospital Manager
Influencers	Head Of Departments
	Staff Specialists or Visiting Medical Officers (Haematology, Vascular)
	Advanced Trainee
	Drug Evaluation committee or Drugs and Therapeutics committee
Recommenders	Chief Pharmacist
Gatekeepers	Procurement Manager
	Lawyer (Contract terms)
End Users	Nurses

In both cases, despite different organisations and different purchases, we can identify the five buying styles. Once we identify the five buying styles, then we can influence them in a way that is more likely to persuade them. So, despite the diversity of titles, we can quickly adapt our persuasion to their buying style. Now we understand how to identify their buying style, we examine how to influence each buying style.

How to influence a buying style

Once you have identified their buying style, then to influence them, you must meet their needs.

The table below summarises how to influence the five buying styles.

BUYING STYLE	HOW TO INFLUENCE THEM
Decision Makers	Focus on results, ROI, cash, profits Show them how to increase performance beyond this financial year Use a high level of structure in meetings You must be credible: • mention key people in their organisation or industry; mention well-known companies you have worked with • prepare and ask great questions
Influencers	Understand their network of stakeholders—try to get referrals from a stakeholder in their network Focus on ideas and people Ask many questions and listen
Recommenders	Be time efficient Build the importance of issues Prepare detailed research on all aspects of the project They value independent data and compliance to standards is important, so refer to standards or specifications Understand the KPIs within their department and the organisation
Gatekeepers	Just as with Decision-makers, enhance your credibility: mention key people in their organisation or industry; mention well-known companies you have worked with Every item, data, dollar is scrutinized, so ensure proposals and documents are accurate Be well prepared and ready to support questions with details: data or evidence Show how your proposals connect with the decision-makers priorities Show them that your idea is better than the status quo
End Users	Needs certainty before the decisions Looking for reliability, so show proven methods or products Prove it is easier to use If possible allow them to trial the product or visit an existing user

The Decision Maker Fallacy

Often in workshops or when consulting, someone asks us "why do I need to bother with anyone except the decision-makers?" Usually, their motivation is to save the time needed to influence the other four buying styles. Our advice is always the same, if you ignore them your persuasion is likely to fail because the other four buying styles will delight in identifying all the problems and challenges with your proposal.

Even if occasionally, you can be successful by just dealing with the decision maker, this short-term success is likely to be temporary because in the long-term it will be undermined by the other buying styles. In contrast, if you engage with each of the buying styles in the way required to influence each style, then your persuasion is more likely to get a YES.

The second major mistake people make around the world is getting to the decision maker or the gatekeeper, too soon. In a perfect world the best order is, first the influencer because they can open doors and get you in front of key people like recommenders. By meeting with influencers, and then recommenders, you arm yourself with the best possible information to persuade the decision-makers. So, unlike many other books, our advice with decision makers is: hasten slowly.

Many of the styles can say no, but cannot say yes to the final decision because they can only recommend yes. Only the decision-makers can give the final YES. However, rarely can you ignore the four buying styles that influence the decision-makers, you must engage and influence these buying styles to ensure long-term and sustained success.

The Consulting Tip

Managing different buying styles is of great importance to differentiating yourself from your competitors, so you need a process to allow you to create a visual map of the different people with their buying styles. In our consulting we use a persuasion map to connect the dots. The buying styles mapping gives you the tools you need to identify the key people. You then decide if you need to connect separately, together, sequentially, by phone, email, etc. and drive mutually beneficial engagement with the customer.

To understand the power of this process, please contact the authors and we will happily share the process.

Insight 10
Influencing Executives: Conduct Effective Executive Interviews

"An executive: someone who has no time to listen to you, and has all the time to talk to you about their business."

Nicholas Read and Dr Stephen Bistritz

Understand Audience	Research Data	Write Close	Write Opening	Structure Content

As discussed in the insight on buying styles, we need to influence decision-makers. For larger or more strategic decisions, those decision-makers will be executives. So, we need to understand how to influence executives.

Why else do we want to influence executives? First, if we want to build a stronger, more strategic relationship with the customer, it is essential to build a relationship with senior executives. Second, if we want to make a big difference to their results we need to move discussions away from price and to more strategic outcomes.

We can influence and persuade executives by effective and structured interviews, where we ask well-planned questions to help the executive think about how changes might affect their business results in future financial years. In a one-to-one or a group presentation, your questions and not your statements, helping executives think about future results, makes you more persuasive to them.

In their 2002 Harvard business review article, Gary Williams and Robert Miller interviewed 1700 executives and identified five thinking and decision styles of executives. So, there are ways we can match the persuasion to meet the needs of their decision-making style. However, before applying this sophisticated approach, first we must clearly understand what interests' executives.

What interest's executives?

Executives are interested in two things—results and changes. Executives are interested in improving the results of their organisation. Executives are also interested in changes outside their organisation that could affect their organisation beyond this current financial year. Typically, these are strategy and long-term planning issues.

Executives are interested in ideas to improve their results. They are not interested in generic ideas but in specific ideas that are tailored to improve their results in their business. We have found a tool from Kim Mauborgne's excellent book, *Blue Ocean strategy* (2005) very useful in thinking about the widest range of results possible. The tool asks four questions; what results can we increase, reduce, eliminate or create? The table below shows some examples of how we can improve results using this tool.

SAMPLES OF WHAT RESULTS CAN WE:	
Increase	Sales
	Inventory turnover
	Margins
	Profits
	Cash flow
	Productivity
Reduce	Operating costs
	Fixed costs
	Variable costs
	Inventory
	Time
Create	New sales
	New customers
	New opportunities
Eliminate	Time
	Work
	Double handling

Another useful tool when thinking about the issues for our customer is to analyse the likely changes in competitive forces in the next three years. Complete a simple table like the one below and write the changes that are likely to affect your customer.

QUESTIONS TO THINK ABOUT THE EXECUTIVE'S BUSINESS	
Over the next three years, what might change with their:	
Customers	Are there likely to be fewer customers, with more power?
	What new channels for customers are opening up, such as the internet?
	What new markets are opening up?
	How are customer needs changing?
Suppliers	Are there likely to be fewer and larger suppliers?
	Are there new low-cost suppliers coming into the market?
Government	Are there likely to be new laws or regulations?
	Will the changes to the law make the barriers to entry for this industry higher or lower?
Substitutes	Could other services or products be substituted for your customer's most profitable product lines?
Competitors	How will the number of competitors change?
	How will the type of competitors change?
New entrants	Could your competitors enter the marketplace? (From overseas or with different business models)
Industry	What changes are expected and will these changes make the industry more or less competitive?
Company	What changes in your customer's organisation are expected?
	What challenges will these changes bring to improving results?

What does not interest executives?

Executives are not interested in your products and services. This is the reason so many people, managers and account managers fail to persuade executives. They do not make the change from talking about products to talking about the key account's results. Partly this is often because this is how they were successful as salespeople—they are comfortable and confident talking about their products and services. Talking about products or services with executives will not get you a meeting, instead you will most likely be referred to the operational side of the organisation.

Talk about financial results

In the beginning, most people are uncomfortable asking questions and talking about financial results. However, it is not hard to ask good questions about financial results.

Any business is simply an investment in assets to produce a profit. So, most executives are interested in increasing their return on assets. Increasing return on assets means improving the most important equation in business:

$$\text{Return on Assets} = \text{Profit} / \text{Assets} = (\text{Profit} / \text{Sales}) \times (\text{Sales}/\text{Assets})$$

For example:

$$\text{Return on Assets} = (7.05\%) \times (1.21) = 8.56\%$$

In simple terms this is: (profit margin) × (how fast you generate cash)

To improve (profit/sales)	Increase margins
	Reduce Operating Costs
	Increase productivity (people and equipment)
To improve (Sales/ Assets)	Increase sales (more customers or more units)
	Improve productivity (machines and buildings)
	Reduce assets
	(get paid earlier, pay later)
	(Increase inventory turnover)

So, the kind of results you should be talking about or asking about are:

- Increasing sales
- Increasing profit (by increasing gross margin or reducing operating costs)
- Increasing productivity (of people, machines or buildings)
- Increasing cash flow

Before you meet: Research the Company

Before seeing an executive, it is essential to research their organisation and to research them. It is becoming much easier to research them using tools like Google and LinkedIn. It is surprising how much public information exists about an executive and the executive's organisation.

Using Google advanced search, you can narrow the search very quickly to a country and also a timescale (for example within a month or a year) in which the executives decisions have been documented.

Using tools like LinkedIn allows you to see who is connected with the executive. It also allows you to see gather information about their experience. Also, interestingly those people who are their connections are good sources of information on topics of conversation.

Before you meet: Prepare great questions

The essence of influencing executives: is asking good questions. Typically as stated earlier, asking questions about possible changes that may affect financial results in the future and asking questions about improving financial results remain the most effective way to deal with executives.

Asking great questions is not necessarily an easy task. To ask great questions you need to create many possible questions and then select the best questions.

Using a structured approach to generating many possible questions is the most effective method for creating a few great questions.

We use a method based on value. In brief, there are three kinds of questions:

Search:	questions to explore where there may be opportunities to deliver value for the executive
Seek:	questions to explore specific opportunities to deliver value for the executive
Satisfy:	questions to explore the consequences and benefits of delivering value in a specific opportunity

As well as generating great questions, you must choose only a few questions because typically you will have no more than 45 min with the executive. So you must choose a few great questions that encourage long answers.

In summary, to influence executives do not focus on your products and services, instead provide insight into changes that may affect their competitive position and provide ideas for improving their business results.

Insight 11
Tailor to Your Target

*"The value of an item must not be based on its price,
but rather on the utility it yields."*

Daniel Bernoulli (1738)

Understand Audience > Research Data > Write Close > Write Opening > Structure Content

Tailor to your target

There is no standard approach to persuading: you must tailor your persuasion approach to your target. If you understand the person you are trying to persuade, then you can adjust your persuasion to suit that person's preferences. A tailored persuasion is more effective and more likely to achieve results.

Different people prefer different language because of their personalities or because they prefer certain behaviour. We can gain insight into their preferences using many different tools, including Myers Briggs (MBTI). We prefer to use the DiSC© system based on behaviour because it is effective, simple and easy to teach. DiSC© is about your personality and behaviour: how you prefer to communicate, what motivates you, what stresses you, how you respond to conflict, and how you solve problems.

DiSC© classifies behaviour into combinations of four types, Dominant, Influencing, Steadiness and Conscientious. DiSC© helps users communicate with each of the four types and can be used for team building, management development and recruitment. For the purposes of this insight we will list some of the differences to demonstrate that each type needs to be persuaded differently.

Dominant and Conscientious people tend to focus on the logic or on the task, whereas Influencing and Steadiness people tend to focus on the people, relationships and emotions. Each of the types has a different perspective on time.

We strongly recommend you use the full DiSC© system when persuading people. However, below we introduce a tool for fast analysis of your persuasion target. This tool will give you a sample of how you can tailor persuasion to your target.

FAST ANALYSIS OF YOUR PERSUASION TARGET TOOL			
How they prefer to communicate:			
Talks more than listens	☐	Listens more than talks	☐
How fast they talk:			
Fast-paced	☐	Slow-paced	☐
How they prefer information:			
Details	☐	Big Picture	☐
How they decide by focusing on:			
Tasks (& facts)	☐	People (& Feelings)	☐
Source: based on some ideas in H. Mills, Artful Persuasion: *How to command attention and change minds and influence people*, p 83.			

Start by assessing yourself. (Force yourself to make a choice between the pairs of preferences, which one is most like you)

1. How do you prefer to communicate: do you talk more than listen or listen more than you talk?
2. How fast do you talk: fast-paced or slow-paced?
3. How do you prefer information: do you prefer details or do you prefer the big picture?
4. How do you decide: by focusing on Tasks (& facts) or by focusing on people (& feelings)?

Once you have answered the questions, plot your choices on the diagram as an X like the example below.

FAST ANALYSIS OF YOUR PERSUASION TARGET TOOL			
How they prefer to communicate:			
Talks more than listens	☒	Listens more than talks	☐
How fast they talk:			
Fast-paced	☒	Slow-paced	☐
How they prefer information:			
Details	☒	Big Picture	☐
How they decide by focusing on:			
Tasks (& facts)	☐	People (& Feelings)	☒

After you have plotted your answers, then answer the same questions about your target.

1. How do they prefer to communicate: do they talk more than listen or listen more than they talk?
2. How fast do they talk: fast-paced or slow-paced?
3. How do they prefer information: do they prefer details or do they prefer the big picture?
4. How do they decide: by focusing on tasks (& facts) or by focusing on people (& feelings)?

Again, force yourself to make a choice between one of the two options, which one is most like them. Again plot your target on the diagram, this time plot as an O so you can see the differences between you and the target.

Often when you do this exercise you will see gaps between how you prefer to work and make decisions and how the target prefers to work and make decisions. In workshops, participants do this exercise on somebody who they find difficult to persuade. The exercise shows them that they are typically two or more areas where they are very different to their target. People naturally prefer to work in ways that are comfortable for them. However if these ways are uncomfortable for the target, then typically you will be unable to persuade the target because you are not working in the way they prefer to work.

In the example below, the persuader with crosses prefers to talk more than listen, talks at a fast pace, talks about details and when deciding focuses on people issues.

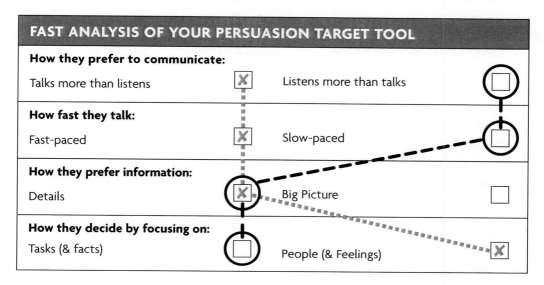

FAST ANALYSIS OF YOUR PERSUASION TARGET TOOL		
How they prefer to communicate:		
Talks more than listens [X]	Listens more than talks [ ]	
How fast they talk:		
Fast-paced [X]	Slow-paced [ ]	
How they prefer information:		
Details [X]	Big Picture [ ]	
How they decide by focusing on:		
Tasks (& facts) [ ]	People (& Feelings) [X]	

In contrast, the target prefers to listen, talks at a slow-pace and when deciding focuses on tasks and facts. While the target does prefer details, these are likely to be details of tasks and facts not details of people.

There are three big gaps between how the persuader prefers to work and how the target prefers to work. If the persuader does not adjust their style to talk less and wait for the target to talk, then they are unlikely to persuade effectively. Also, if they do not change their persuasion to include tasks and facts instead of their own preference for people and feelings, then again their persuasion is likely to be ineffective.

Once we understand the type of our target then we can begin to adjust our communication style to better suit how they prefer to work. The table below shows how we can adjust to suit the target style.

With someone who: Talks more than listens	**With someone who: Listens more than talks**
• Let them talk, and think out loud	• Ask, then listen carefully
• Include a variety of topics	• Talk about one thing at a time
• Communicate verbally	• Communicate in writing, if possible
• Expect immediate action	• Give them adequate time to reflect

With someone who prefers information: details	With someone who prefers information: big picture
• State topic clearly • Prepare facts and examples • Present information step-by-step • Stress practical applications • Finish your sentences • Draw on past, real examples • Talk about the details • Provide them with dossiers of data and detailed references to study later	• Talk about the principles and key ideas • Talk about the "big picture" and its implications • Talk about possibilities • Use analogies and metaphors • Brainstorm Options • Engage their imaginations • Don't overwhelm them with details
How they decide by focusing on: logic and facts	**How they decide by focusing on: people and feelings**
• Be organized and logical • Consider the cause and effect • Focus on consequences • Don't ask how they 'feel'; ask what they 'think' • Appeal to their sense of fairness • Don't repeat yourself	• First mention points of agreement • Appreciate their efforts and contributions • Recognise legitimacy of feelings • Talk about "people" concerns • Smile and maintain good eye contact • Be friendly and considerate

People are persuaded by different language

Another set of preferences comes from how people use their brains to process thoughts. Skilled counsellors can identify some preferences using Neuro-linguistic Programming (NLP). For the business world, Sue Knight provides a readable and practical introduction in her book *NLP at Work*. We will discuss:

- VAK—visual, auditory and kinaesthetic (see, hear and experience)
- Same, different
- Towards, away from

We all have a preference for either visual, auditory or kinaesthetic—each of us prefers to see, hear or experience. Often the quickest way to identify our preference is to listen:

- **Visual** people might say: "I see what you mean" or "We need to look at the key issues" or "I don't like the look of that."
- **Auditory** people might say: "I hear what you are saying" or "I don't like the sound of that" or "We need to ensure everyone is singing the same tune."

- **Kinaesthetic** people might say: "I have a bad feeling about this" or "We need to try it out" or "We need to keep digging until we get to the bottom of this."

We all use some of these phrases some of the time however, we tend to prefer one of the three types over the others: visual, auditory or kinaesthetic. Imagine you are trying to describe two companies working together in a strategic alliance. Depending on the preference of the listener you might say:

- "I see us looking out into the market to find the best opportunities."
- "I hear us singing the same song to the market."
- "I can imagine us shoulder to shoulder fighting the competition in the market."

Another preference division is 'same or different', where some people look for what is similar while others look for the differences. Again you might describe a new computer system in two ways:

- "It is similar to the old one, without the weaknesses."
- "It is different to the old system. We have taken a fresh approach and used a new design."

Finally some people like to 'move away from things' and some 'move towards things'. Both can be satisfied with something like, "The new system leaves behind the problems of the past and allows us to move towards the opportunities in the future. If you use the phrase "from ... to", this covers both frames.

Getting Better

Sometimes people say to us "Using different language for different people is too complex. I do not have time for this". We suggest that once you are aware that there are differences in behaviour or personality that influence the language they prefer, you become more sensitive about choosing language. If you begin to listen for the differences or ask questions about the person you want to persuade, you will be amazed at how easily you find the language people prefer. For example if we are going to meet a potential client we ask four questions to someone who has dealt with that person:

- Tell me about this person?
- Do they prefer to talk or prefer to listen?
- Do they prefer the 'big picture' or more detail?
- Do they focus on logic or people, on facts or feelings?

Their answers are sufficient for you to choose a language.

To improve your skills at adapting language for different preferences, just listen. The next time you are in a meeting, take in a list of some preferences and record how many different preferences you can identify. Once you are aware of preferences, pick one person and try talking to them using their preferences. People typically find their conversation is more lively and friendly than before because matching the other person's preferences creates a strong rapport.

Insight 12
Consider Culture

ISRAEL

*"Resolving conflict is rarely about who is right.
It is about acknowledgment and appreciation of the differences."*

Thomas F Crum

Understand Audience	Research Data	Write Close	Write Opening	Structure Content

The business world is getting smaller and smaller. More and more people are presenting in foreign countries, to people from backgrounds different to their own. Being aware of cultural sensitivities is part of understanding the audience's needs and is just as important in your own country as it is when you are abroad. Language is not the only potential challenge. Audience members might also have different views on power, hierarchy, gender, age, status, group interaction and participation.

Prior to planning to persuade a foreign audience, we suggest that you research the cultural differences. Overlooking subtle variations can lead to a misunderstanding of your message and may even offend the audience. As you present outside your country, find out what the differences are so your message is not discarded because you opened your session with an insult when you thought you were being clever.

Finding the Information

We recommend an excellent book called *Kiss, Bow, or Shake Hands* by Terri Morrison, Wayne Conaway and George Borden. This book lists countries alphabetically and provides a review of the culture, business practices and protocols for each.

Second, for more information on a particular culture, read a travel guide or look at a website like www.lonelyplanet.com. We also suggest trying the government's web site or even the embassy or consulate. There is a list of the world's embassies at www.embassyworld.com.

Third, for online training and information visit Culture Wizard at http://rw-3.com.

Language Barriers

Culture means different things to different people. However, the obvious cultural difference is in the application and understanding of language.

International presenters know that interpreters are a necessary part of presenting in a foreign land. You should be aware that when giving a presentation using an interpreter, your message may be distorted. The audience will interpret the message through the interpreter, as well as through your tone and body language.

You might be able to minimise the distortion if you brief the interpreter before the presentation, but some distortion is inevitable. To at least maximise the impact of your own body language, make sure you address the audience rather than the person who is translating your message. Sometimes it is hard to resist the urge to speak to the person who actually understands what you are saying, but you should try.

Even if you are using a translator, most people will appreciate your attempt to say a few words in their language. Saying hello, goodbye and thank you in Chinese has helped us build rapport with a technical audience of Chinese engineers. However, if you are not a fluent speaker of the language, be careful that you get it right! Some readers will recall the story of President Kennedy giving an address in Berlin, where he announced, "Ich bin ein Berliner", which means, "I am a jam filled donut". He had meant to say, "Ich bin Berliner", meaning, "I am a Berliner".

More likely though, you will be presenting in English to a foreign audience that knows English as a second language. Unless the audience is fluent, you should:

- Keep your language simple.
- Clarify your points.
- Speak more slowly and deliberately (without being patronising).
- Avoid slang and colloquialisms.

- Use visual aids, such as handouts or PowerPoint® slides—Learners of any foreign language will know that it is much easier to understand a concept by reading about it than listening to it being described.
- Consider having sub-titles on your slides or handouts—'Dual language' slides will clear up any misunderstandings, as seen in parts of Canada, where the English and French language on signs and products.
- Use lots of pictures that have universal meanings.

Differences Across Cultures

Culture will influence every part of your presentation; from the way you dress to how you conduct breaks. In France, for example, lunch is a much grander affair than in many other parts of the world. The French often enjoy a three-course meal over lunch, with a two-hour break. A French audience may not be too pleased if you only schedule a thirty-minute lunch break for sandwiches.

"Hello", "Bonjour" or "Konnichiwa"?

Something you will have to deal with during an overseas business trip is how to greet foreign acquaintances. While the Western world is used to a handshake, other cultures often use a different form of greeting. Many cultures are well versed in Western customs, and will most likely greet a Westerner with a handshake. However, this may not always be the case, so it is best to learn the traditional greeting.

Learning the greeting will show your foreign audience that you respect their customs and are open minded enough to have an interest in their culture. The traditional greeting may be a bow or even a kiss. You will need to find out the particulars of the greeting, such as how far you should bow, as in some cultures this symbolises status.

Introductions

Every culture differs in how titles are used. Sound advice is to follow other people's prompts. Some cultures require full titles, while others will be quick to use first names.

In Australia, listing credentials and using a formal title is seen as an individual decision. The author Stephen has no credentials on his card, whereas Gary needs a much larger card to cover all his credentials. However, in East Asian cultures, social standing is highly significant, and as a presenter you should assume authority and not try to create an air of familiarity.

Another consideration is that body language is not universal, so be careful about hand gestures, such as pointing, making a fist or giving the thumbs up sign.

For example, while direct eye contact in Australia and North America is custom, it can be considered rude and invasive in some cultures.

Respecting the Culture

Every culture has a stereotype, which is a product of ignorance. Look for and respond to individual differences rather than stereotypes. When Persuading For Results, your role is to understand the culture you are presenting to, and to understand your audience.

Finally, consider the values of the culture you are presenting in. You need to respect the beliefs and customs of the audience members and consider your behaviour, clothing and the content of your presentation.

Insight 13
Research, Research, Research

"Chance favours a prepared mind."
Louis Pasteur

| Understand Audience | **Research Data** | Write Close | Write Opening | Structure Content |

Never underestimate the importance of research. When Persuading for Results, thorough and up-to-date information helps persuade an audience. In contrast, the Basic Presenter will rely on old research, presenting the same information they presented ten years ago. Old research is less persuasive to an audience.

If the audience feels you are overlooking a crucial piece of information, they will doubt your credibility, and when it comes to question time, you may find yourself backed into a corner. Remember, before you can talk about a topic you need to become an expert in it. Gathering the relevant information can sometimes seem to take forever, but it is a crucial element of presentation preparation. Begin by reading broadly about the subject and then focus your research on more specific points.

Books

Books will provide you with a solid overview. Books often summarise the history of a subject, review different thoughts on the topic, and expose a broad range of ideas. We recommend that you read any books considered 'landmarks' for your topic.

For example, no one should present on evolution without having read Charles Darwin's *The Origin of Species*.

However, never limit your research to books. They may take years to write and publish, so even a recent book may not report the latest findings on a subject. The key is to complement books with journals.

Journals

Journals are an excellent source of information. Journal articles are particularly good for presenting in areas of science, technology and business, as they will give you the latest research that books simply can not provide. A journal article usually outlines a very specific piece of research, which can be very useful for supporting a particular point.

For example, www.medlink.com is a medical journal. If you were presenting on the affect of marijuana on the brain, this would be an ideal journal where you could search for a specific study related to your topic, by searching for key words, such as 'cannabis and brain'.

While some websites will give you access to journals, periodicals and newspaper articles, they generally charge a fee to download. You can pay to use these websites or you can visit a public library to use their database of journal and newspaper articles. Large libraries usually have hard copies of journals, as well as electronic copies. Using these resources will ensure that your information is up to date.

There are many journals to draw from, but here is a list of some sites to give you a start:

- Harvard Business Review is particularly relevant for presentations about business issues, such as leadership and teamwork (www.harvardbusinessonline.hsbc.harvard.edu).
- The American Psychological Association has a database called 'PsycInfo'. It offers a wealth of articles from a large database of psychological journals, although there is a hefty subscription fee (www.psycinfo.com).
- The Australian Institute of Management provides a database of articles for members—another great resource for business related topics (www.aimnet.com.au).
- In Australia, *Business Review Weekly* is a great source for business articles (www.brw.com.au). Also the *Australian Financial Review* often has good articles about issues for businesses and industries (www.afr.com.au).

University and library websites usually provide a comprehensive list of their journals. It is well worth taking advantage of your local university's resources.

The Internet

Have a look at *Insight 14—Become a Digital Detective,* for some tips on how to become a Digital Detective.

Using an Expert

Have you ever experienced that sinking feeling when you have been asked to present on a topic that you are totally unfamiliar with? No matter what you do, that knot in your stomach just gets tighter and tighter.

In these situations it is sometimes more appropriate to seek out an expert in that field. In doing so, you may like to first of all consider how you wish to work with the selected person.

The key question is: must *you* do the presentation? If the answer is no, you may decide to delegate the entire task of researching, writing and delivering the presentation to the expert. If the answer is yes, you will only be able to delegate the research and writing. Alternatively, you may consider sharing the stage with your expert, calling on them to speak only during parts of the presentation. In any case, you should develop an understanding of the topic and the expert will help you with this.

If you would like to meet with an expert but do not know anyone appropriate, ask around. Having a contact will make it easier to arrange an appointment. Otherwise, you might have to make several telephone calls to find the right person to speak to.

When you ask the expert if you can meet to discuss a topic, be clear about the reason for your request and how long you would like to meet for. Since they are doing you a favour, try to make it as convenient as possible for them.

The expert will have no problem divulging a wealth of information—everyone loves to be asked his or her opinion and there is nothing better than an eager listener. Jot down notes and make sure you are clear about any points they bring up. Ask them for any advice on where you should seek further information. Thank them for their time and after the presentation, send them a thank you note to tell them how the presentation went.

Build Your Library

It is useful to develop your own library. If you are a regular speaker on a particular topic you may have already collected many books on the subject. Over the years, we have acquired dozens of books on each of the topics we present on. We have found it useful to categorise these on our bookshelves and we have created our own library database. This way we can save time by searching for books quickly on our database. Also, when we lend a book to a key audience member, we keep track of the loan in our database.

We suggest that you systematically record and file any printed notes. Organise your speaking files by subjects, such as the topics you present in, and then other general resources such as pictures, quotes and stories. You will thank yourself for such pragmatic planning when you begin preparation for your next presentation.

RESEARCHING THE DATA TOOL: COLOSSAL SPORTS	
What are the key books relating to your topic?	*Every Business is a Growth Business: How your company can prosper year after year* by Ram Charan and Noel Tichy. *Profitable Growth is Everyone's Business: 10 tools you can use Monday morning* by Ram Charan. *The Alchemy of Growth: Practical insights for building the enduring enterprise* by Merhdad Baghai, Stephen Coley, David White. *Using Technology to Move Forward* by Simone Kelly.
What are some relevant journals to use as a resource?	The Sports Journal of Technology. The Institute of Profits Monthly Periodical.
What are some web sites that you should look at?	Our competitors. Deloitte Fast 50 — high growth companies. Search for some innovative companies.
Is there someone in particular that you should interview for information?	Richard Robinson, CEO of Bloom Consulting, the most successful engineering firm in the world. His company is constantly redeveloping their computer system and encouraging innovation. They have a rigorous measuring system, tracking not only financials but also employee and client satisfaction. Bloom Consulting is a great case study for this project.
Do you have any existing notes on the topic?	Notes from seminars on IT for high-growth companies. Notes on how to implement new information systems.
Are there any other sources that you think could be useful?	Technical information from the IT department. The managers would be persuaded by talking to managers who have implemented the same system.

RESEARCHING THE DATA TOOL: COMMUNITY GARDEN

What are the key books relating to your topic?	*Getting Started In Community Gardening—A guide to planning, designing and implementation of community garden projects* *Public Produce; The new urban agriculture* (2009) by D. Nordahl *Greening Cities, Growing Communities* by Hou, Johnson & Lawson
What are some relevant journals to use as a resource?	Australian City Farms and Community Gardens Network Community Harvest magazine
What are some web sites that you should look at?	Cultivating communities Good Practise Guide www.communitygarden.org.au
Do you have any existing notes on the topic?	Yes—Permaculture Design Course texts
Are there any other useful sources?	Videos on composting and waste management that can be given/lent to council members.

Insight 14
Become a Digital Detective

"Any fool can make things bigger and more complex... it takes a touch of genius and a lot of courage to move it the opposite direction."

Albert Einstein

Understand Audience | **Research Data** | Write Close | Write Opening | Structure Content

Thanks to technology, you have quick and easy access to an abundance of information. In 2008, it was estimated the world was generating as much unique information in one year as in the previous 5000 years. Also, the amount of technical information is doubling every two years. In the face of this digital tsunami of information, you need to become a digital detective. To help you become a digital detective, we explain *How To Find Good Evidence On The Internet*, *How To Find Good Evidence On Your Hard Drive (Or Network)* and then show you, *How To Keep Your Evidence Up-To Date Quickly*.

How to find good evidence on the internet

The Internet is an invaluable research tool for any persuasive presenter. However, it is vital to distinguish between useful information and rubbish. So you need to become a digital detective. If you are going to use data from a website to support your presentation, ensure a credible institution, such as a university or government body, supports the site. If you are unfamiliar with using the Internet for research, ask a colleague or your local librarian (or your kids) to help you.

Most presenters have not been trained in how to search the Internet effectively. We learned a great deal from a company established by two librarians who combine the expertise of librarians with the power of the Internet (www. enterpriseinformation.com.au).

Different search engines give you different results and Metasearch engines search a combination of search engines. For information on different search engines have a look at www.searchenginesshowdown.com.

When we research, we rely on a few sites that provide access to relevant articles. As with obtaining electronic journals, most of these require becoming a member and paying to download each article, but some give free access.

Here are a few sites that we find particularly useful:

- Comprehensive information on any country from The CIA World Fact book: www.cia.gov/library/publications/the-world-factbook/index.html.
- Thousands of newspapers from around the world are available at www. onlinenewspapers.com.
- American news sites include www.cnn.com, www.economist.com and www.nytimes.com.
- Australian news sites include: The Fairfax website (www.fairfax.com. au) offers access to Australian newspapers and magazines, including the Sydney Morning Herald, The Age, Business Review Weekly and the Financial Review; the News Limited site at www.news.com.au; The Australian Broadcasting Commission (ABC) at www.abc.net.au.
- Statistics can be found at www.abs.gov.au, the site for the Australian Bureau of Statistics. For American statistics go to www.census.gov.
- Minerals history and economics, US geological survey: minerals.usgs.gov
- A portal with many links for business www.ceoexpress.com
- Quotes can be found at www.great-quotes.com.

Use Advanced Searching

Learn how to use the advanced search features, as these can speed up your search and narrow down the selection quickly. Using a search engine like www.google.com and searching for key words is also a good way to gain a lot of information. The more words you type into the Google search box, then the more likely you are to get relevant results. For example, type in "persuading" and you will find 337 million results. However, type in "persuading your bank manager to give you a bank loan" and this reduces dramatically to 207,000.

Google search results now offer the opportunity to narrow down your results quickly; on the left hand side of your screen of Google results, you should see icons for Images, video and news. But hidden at the bottom of the list is a phrase—more search tools. Click on "More search tools" and you will find a range of tools that allow you to narrow down your search very quickly. The most useful of these is to be able to narrow down your results to a particular time period: latest, past 24 hours, past week, past month, past year or custom time period. We find filtering results by past month or by past year is a quick way to find the most current information.

Using Google's advanced search page will often reduce a list of 40,000 down to a few hundred. If you look on the bottom right hand side of the standard Google search box, there is a link which says advanced search. If you click on *Advanced Search*, this takes you to the Google advanced search page. This search page allows you to narrow down your search to specific terms. Also it allows you to exclude terms. So, if you search for "persuasion" you will get more than 12 million hits. However, you notice many of these refer to Jane Austen's novel persuasion. Using advanced search, in the box called *don't show pages that have... any of these unwanted words* **add**: "Jane Austen", persuasion, novel. Excluding pages with these words reduces the hits from 12 million to 2 million and you start to see more relevant searches.

Also, with advanced searching, you can search for a particular kind of document like a PowerPoint® file or a PDF. The results of a search for files like PowerPoint® will show existing presentations. Seeing how other people have presented can help you prepare much faster.

With the abundance of information available on the Internet, and being able to search effectively and also knowing where specialist sites are is a critical skill. We recommend Maureen Henninger's book The *Hidden Web: Finding Quality Information On The Net*, that includes detailed information on searching for specific subject areas and identifies specialist sites.

How To Find Good Evidence On Your Hard Drive (Or your Network)

Build a digital Library

As well as building a personal library, it is also useful to store information on your computer system. Organised computer files are an excellent resource. For example, on our computer files, we have downloaded articles, and saved links to our favourite web sites. This careful organisation might seem time consuming, but in the long run it saves time and stress.

We suggest that you systematically record and file any printed notes. Organise your speaking files by subjects, such as the topics you present in, and then other general resources such as pictures, quotes and stories. You will thank yourself for such pragmatic planning when you begin preparation for your next presentation.

Get Bill Gates to help you

We recognise that systematic record management is easier for some than others. Therefore, we suggest always keeping your notes in electronic format. Even if you do not have a well-organised system, Bill Gates can help you. On all versions of Windows there are *Search* functions, usually near the *Start* button or in the control panel. Typically this allows you to search the contents of the file, type of file or file modification dates. If you have a few clues, then the computer will find it for you.

Beyond the simple windows search tool, as the amount of information explodes our challenge is to find the best information, fast. All of us are faced with the challenge of doing more in less time.

Better Than Bill Gates

Google Desktop offers a free tool that offers some search capabilities but also slows down your computer.

Much faster than Windows, and more powerful than Google Desktop, is professional search software like ISYS workgroup (http://www.isys-search.com). This software quickly indexes all forms of documents (and databases) on your computer, in less than an hour for most users and then will answer any query in less than a second. Apart from the speed, it has sophisticated search options (e.g. "in the same paragraph as", "within 10 words of", "followed anywhere by" and "in the paragraph labelled") these search options mean you can find what you are looking for much faster.

As experienced searchers, we appreciate other features that speed up our work including being able to narrow the search results by limiting the date of the document by dragging a cursor to show your date range. Also, narrowing the list by just looking at one type of document or in one directory with a few mouse clicks. Our favourite is being able to search within the current results, because having seen the first results we can usually sharpen our search and find what we want by just searching within the results. This is the way we use more often, rather than spending time building a sophisticated and precise query. We think of it as like panning for gold, the first query is a rough sieve to get rid of most of the unwanted material. Then by searching again just within results of the first search, its like passing the material through a much finer sieve—that's when we find the gold, the article or information we are searching for.

Professional search software can also index documents across a network. Imagine you are Persuading For Results with a major customer and need to find the latest information. However, this information is scattered across different departments and different locations in the country. With professional software, you could see all the documents within five seconds. You could search another index of emails and in 5 seconds see all the customer emails in the last month. Armed with the latest information, you need not worry about the latest customer issues someone forgot to tell you and you would be a more persuasive presenter.

When Persuading For Results, we all face the challenge of doing more in less time, Professional searching can save you hours and help you be more persuasive by finding up-to-date information, fast.

How To Keep Your Evidence Up-To Date Quickly

To Persuade for Results you must have fresh, contemporary information. We all need to keep informed in the most effective and fastest method. A couple of quick ways of keeping up-to-date are to use ALLTOP and to use Google Reader.

ALLTOP is a site that collects together information from many different sites. Currently, the sites are in several groups: Work, Health, Culture, Interests, Tech, People, Good, News, Geos and Sports. If you click on *Work*, then this takes you to a list of topics from accounting to web conferencing. If you click on speaking, you will see on one page the 5 titles of the most recent posts from more than 75 sites. You can quickly scan the titles and click on the ones that interest you. ALLTOP allows you to set up an account and customise what you see to make seeing information even faster. This technique is much faster than surfing the internet hoping to find a good source of information.

A second technique is to use Google Reader. The quickest way to understand this is to watch a one minute video on YouTube—Google Reader in Plain English. In simple terms decide on the websites you want to monitor and the latest updates appear in Google Reader. They can appear in list view, so you can scan the titles very quickly and only click and read the interesting or relevant entries.

This means you can monitor many websites in one place and is an efficient way to keep up-to-date. We currently use Reader to monitor 145 different websites. One practical tip is to collect similar sites into folders, that way you can review similar websites at the same time and see similarities and trends. So we don't see 145 subscriptions but see 12 groups. It's easy to add or delete website as your interests change. You can use Google Reader to monitor an ALLTOP page like speaking which is monitoring 75 sites. So, this makes keeping up to date very efficient. The best news of all is that Google Reader is free, all you need to do is create a Google account.

Up-to-date information will make you more persuasive. Using these tools you will find up-to-date information fast and you can save hours when researching—why not use the time saved to make your presentation even more persuasive?

Insight 15
Closing

*"We are judged by what we finish,
not by what we start."*

| Understand Audience | Research Data | **Write Close** | Write Opening | Structure Content |

When Persuading for Results, the two most important stages of the presentation are the close and the opening. Audience members tend to concentrate and to remember these short sections of your presentation. However, many presenters do not spend enough time on these critical stages. This is usually because the presenter has only a small amount of preparation time left for the close, because of spending too much time on the content. This is why we suggest that you write the close first. Other authors, including David Peoples, agree. This is because it helps focus your attention on the outcome you want from the presentation and makes you more ruthless when culling content.

The close is your opportunity to leave a positive parting impression. The close stage will go more smoothly if you follow a set procedure. The suggestions offered for this stage offer you plenty of flexibility, while assisting you to close effectively.

Judging from our experience, we believe you will save between 30% and 50% of your preparation time if you write the close first.

Signal your close

People are always happier with some sort of map. At the end of the content stage, you should recap the main points. Then you should tell the audience that the presentation will conclude shortly. The words you use may vary, but you could say something like, "We have got ten minutes left. There are three points I would like to leave you with" or "It is time to wind things up, but just before we do,"—then lean forward and get ready for a powerful close.

Summarise main points

The close is an opportunity for you to reiterate your key points to check for understanding. At this stage it is not appropriate to introduce new material, as it will detract from your message. Instead, give a simple and succinct summary of the main points.

Make a Statement of Reality

A 'statement of reality' is a closing statement that reinforces the connection between your presentation and the challenges facing the audience. Ideally it should centre on the experiences of the audience and the subject of your presentation. It might be something like, "Today's presentation dealt with the challenges of building teams. This is important to everyone here because your company is making you responsible for building teams. You are all equipped with the knowledge to do this effectively, but your success will depend on whether you turn this knowledge into practice."

Explain what ACTION is required

At the end of a presentation, when Persuading For Results you want the audience to take some form of action. Do you want them to buy the product or service? Do you want them to support your proposal? Do you want them to implement your ideas in their workplace? Whatever it is, make it clear. Most presentations that fail at this point do so because nobody is sure what is required of them. Be clear, concise and specific.

To Persuade, Close with impact

Making an impact does not mean you have to thump the podium or shout. A whisper can have a greater impact than a shout. There are many ways to close with impact, including using a final anecdote, a quote from a famous figure, a quiet, rhetorical question or a motivational statement such as "You are about to take a giant step forward…". We suggest you consider combining your closing words with a visual to help the audience remember your final message.

Your close should always be positive and empowering. Even if you spent the last hour explaining why sales, productivity and morale are at an all time low, send the audience off determined to do something to change the situation. Be positive and persuasive and give them a reason to take action.

Sometimes just switch off

Sometimes the most powerful way to close is switch off the projector or put on a black slide and then say your closing words. One of the authors remembers the first time he used a black slide with an audience of 150. As the screen went black, 150 pairs of eyes moved from the screen to him, just waiting for the final words. He took a deep breath, paused and then spoke the final words to a riveted audience. It was a convincing lesson on the power of the black slide to direct the audience's attention to the presenter for the crucial closing words.

Make yourself available

If your presentation is promoting your products or services, you should make your materials and yourself available after the presentation. Tell the audience how to contact you if they wish to discuss any issues with you later.

THE CLOSE TOOL: COLOSSAL SPORTS	
Duration	12 minutes
How will you signal your close?	I will use the image of a team white-water rafting again to suggest we are all in this together.
	I will say, "My final comments will be brief, but they will bring together our discussions over the last 2 hours and will have enormous benefits for our business future."
How will you summarise your main points?	I will summarise the key issues.
	"There are four key issues to think about. First, The board wants to grow profits. Second, the system will help all divisions grow their profits in different ways. Third, we are unlikely to lose another Marbella because of our systems. Finally, the system has the flexibility to meet our needs now and in the future."

What is your 'statement of reality'?	"The system will be easier for everyone to use, teams will be motivated and profitability will continue to improve. We as an executive team will not be embarrassed again in front of the board and you can make strategic decisions without worrying which accounts are about to defect."
What action is required from the audience?	"I need you to approve the budget expenditure so the research stage and project scope can start at the beginning of next month."
How will you close with impact?	"The image on the screen shows a raft on white water, with the words 'the future belongs to our team'. Our decision today will help all of us benefit from this technology, and more importantly, it will allow our customers to receive the level of service from us that they deserve."

THE CLOSE TOOL: COMMUNITY GARDEN

Duration	10 minutes
How will you signal your close?	I will show a slide of the image of a discontented, multi-demographic community standing in between their high rise apartments. Evidently, from the photo there will be no room to grow anything. I will say, 'My final comments will be brief, but will further highlight the importance and value of this community garden.'
How will you summarise your main points?	I will summarise the key issues, being that the community wants this garden; it will benefit council as it will promote community spirit. Also, Council's reputation and popularity will increase as well as promoting a healthy lifestyle for the community.
What is your 'statement of reality'?	"A community garden will enhance the sustainability of our community. It will also encourage a community spirit and promote a healthy lifestyle".
What action is required from the audience?	Approve and support the community garden, commit to some funding and set up of the garden and allocate of the plot of land.
How will you close with impact?	The final image will be of another preexisting community garden in a similar area. The people will be happy alongside abundant fruit and vegetables.

Insight 16
Opening

"Rather than close a sale, open a relationship."

Cathy De Vrye

> Understand Audience > Research Data > Write Close > **Write Opening** > Structure Content >

As we mentioned in the previous Insight, when Persuading For Results the two most important parts of the presentation are the close and the opening. After designing the close, you need to design the opening. This stage involves creating a title, setting the scene, connecting with the audience, making a benefit statement and giving a sneak preview of what is to come. The opening stage is crucial in establishing your topic, your credibility and your relationship with the audience. To help you start with impact we will examine some key elements to consider, then focus on the process.

Before the event

If you are comfortable on your feet already, research and our experience shows that most people are anxious in the first 3–5 minutes. So, we recommend that everything that you can do to help the audience want to come to your meeting/ presentation is critical. Here are some things for you to focus on and prepare before the big day.

A title with impact

The first step is to develop a presentation title that will hook your audience. The title should give some insight into the content of your presentation. It should promise new insights and should be concise and where possible creative.

For example, you might start with the topic, 'Increasing Sales'. A more promising title is 'Ten Ways to Increase Sales.' By adding just one word to the title it becomes 'Ten Creative Ways to Increase Sales'. For added interest, 'Back flips, Handstands and Ten Other Creative Ways to Increase Sales.'

For a recent Permaculture presentation, "Cities feeding themselves—a new direction in community gardens."

Pace

Think carefully about your audience when you decide how to connect with them. Some will respond well to a fast-paced start, while others will feel more comfortable with a chatty, laid-back approach.

If your presentation is designed to get people to interact, you might ask them to get up and move around. While some people dislike having to mingle, it does help break down barriers between people. You might ask people to complete a quick quiz and compare answers with those around them. You may ask people to discuss a hypothetical situation in groups of three and then compare answers with another group of three.

If you pose a question, present the question on a slide. This avoids questions from the audience such as, "Can you remind us what we are supposed to be doing?"

Delivering your Opening with Impact

The big day has arrived and you want the selected executives to approve your project. If your meeting starts at 10am, be there at 9am, check everything. Then you have the capacity to set the scene as you're audience arrives.

Don't still be bent over the computer making a last minute change, instead greet and engage them so your presence will let them know you are prepared and ready to produce results.

Setting the scene

As people begin to enter the room, the atmosphere will influence their mood and their view of you and of the presentation. Therefore, it is important to create the right atmosphere from the outset.

Setting the scene can be as simple as playing music or displaying a picture on an overhead as people walk in. You might choose a beautiful beach scene to help the audience switch their minds away from the demands of the workplace, leaving them with a fresh attitude to the presentation. Alternatively, you might choose a photograph linked to the presentation topic, to focus the audience's attention.

Introduction

Even though you will often have audiences that know you well, always have someone else introduce you. So if you are part of the executive team, have the most senior person in the room introduce and share your credentials on this project with the team.

We suggest writing a few lines for the person, this will enhance your credibility and keep them on track. If you let people waffle, they could destroy your presentation by taking a different view at the start.

Connect with the Audience

There are many different ways to begin a presentation so you connect with the audience. Your choice depends on your message and the composition of your audience. Remember, there is nothing like enthusiasm to motivate the audience, and immediately help them warm to you. Make your whole attitude say, "I am glad to be here and I have great news for you! You cannot afford not to know this."

The aim should always be the same—grab the audience's attention and get them involved. Consider using one of the following methods:

- A story
- A rhetorical question
- A joke
- An arresting fact
- A quotation

A story

Telling a personal story to lead into the first point can help capture the audience's attention. A personal story will connect you with your audience and make listeners feel like you are sharing yourself with them. They will like you more as you become more 'real' and personable.

It is best if the story relates the interests and needs of your audience. If you do tell a story, avoid casting yourself into the leading role if you were not present at the event. Presentation veterans will understand the frustration of having heard half a dozen different presenters tell the same story, each featuring them self as the main character. We will discuss the power of stories again in *Insight 34—Tell Stories*.

An arresting fact

An arresting fact can act as a way to startle your audience into attention. It will grab their interest and give your topic credibility. You may begin your presentation on protecting native wildlife with, "Eighteen of Australia's native mammals have become extinct since European settlement." The audience will be intrigued to know more.

A rhetorical question

A rhetorical question will get the audience thinking about your topic. It will involve them as they relate their own experience to what you are talking about. For example, if you are about to talk about expressing emotions, you could begin with "When was the last time you told a friend that you love them?"

A quotation

The quotation is another effective way to grab the audience's attention, while introducing your topic. Quoting an authority or well-respected person will give your topic some credibility and is also interesting. As with all types of beginnings, ensure that your quotation is relevant to your presentation.

Problems and opportunities

Most of the audience will be asking themselves two questions: "Why am I here?" and "What is in it for me?" However, it can be effective to let people discover problems or opportunities for themselves. We suggest asking good questions and then pausing to let the audience consider the answers. When done well, this process can engage the audience and give them a sense of participating in the journey towards a solution.

Jokes

Take care when using jokes. In fact, we recommend that you do not use jokes at all because while there are many jokes, there are very few gifted joke-tellers. If you are not usually good at telling jokes, or usually fluff the punch line, don't attempt it. You want your audience laughing with you, not at you.

If you do decide to tell a joke, choose carefully so that it will not offend anyone in the audience and keep it short and punchy. Also, look for something different. If you have heard the joke more than once, the audience has probably heard it too. For more on jokes, see *Insight 38—Using Humour*.

What action: Tell them in a sentence.

Even though you will do many presentations, our focus in this book is on how you can persuade for results.

This part of your opening must be delivered with focus and clarity. Rehearse this part, be confident and be clear with what you want the audience to do at the end of your session.

Do you want them to approve your project, provide funding or start a research project? Whatever it is, tell them in a single sentence. The trap here is to waffle and to try to do a big sell. It does not work, get their attention and then provide tangible benefits.

Benefit Statement: Why should they listen?

As well as connecting with the audience, the opening must include a benefit statement. A benefit statement is a brief account of the reasons why the audience should listen to you. In the planning stage, you thought about why the audience needs your input. Now is the time to turn those reasons into a benefit statement that explains what you hope the audience will take from the presentation. Your statement should outline the expected benefits explicitly.

You could say something like "I am going to show you six ways that are guaranteed to get your clients to telephone you." Or, "We are going to identify the four things that will turn customers away." Don't forget to tell them why this matters. For example, "I am going to show you how to reduce your operating costs by 20%. The *benefit* of that to your business is increased profit and extra resources to pursue new business opportunities."

Use concrete examples. For example, if the audience understands that they can have a 20% increase in productivity, sales or profit, they will listen more carefully to your presentation.

Sneak Preview

Give the audience a glimpse of the presentation ahead. Learn from the all-time top movies: Titanic, Star Wars and Avatar. Your preview should be like a movie trailer, intriguing your audience and generating interest in your presentation.

If you have something more controversial, tell the group early in the process that you are intending to share some facts before they make their final decision. This will keep them open to your presentation as you present the facts.

A sneak preview should give a brief overview of the structure of the presentation and allow the audience to look forward to what you have planned. For example, you might like to say something like, "For the next twenty minutes, I am going to talk to you about our strategy for the forthcoming year. Then I will show you a new interview with our CEO. Following this, we are going to divide into groups and discuss the video."

Incorporating Permaculture

As previously discussed, the growing importance of sustainability and conservation is permeating through society and Permaculture offers practical, sustainable solutions. In the opening of your presentation use a title that immediately captures the audience's attention, for example 'Affordable and Sustainable solutions for your Business, Family and Community'. With a title like this the target audience see how Permaculture can apply to all aspects of life and reiterates the affordability of moving to a more sustainable lifestyle. It is important to consider how you will deliver and connect with the audience when introducing ideas about Permaculture as it can easily be misconstrued as a 'hippy' concept which affects the audience's perception of the content. Therefore, it is important to perceive what the audience already understands and believe. To gain this perception you could create a hypothetical situation which groups could discuss, or show images of degraded farms compared with Permaculture farms to show the contrast. Another idea is to show how recent environmental legislation limits community and individuals from moving toward a more sustainable lifestyle. Above all your opening should be arresting and inspiring, you want your audience to be excited about the information and practical tools that they are about to hear.

THE OPENING TOOL: COLOSSAL SPORTS

Presentation title	Conquering Colossal Rapids: Our Journey Towards Success
Duration	15 minutes
How will you 'set the scene' for the audience arrival? (Music, picture, beverages available, meet and greet.)	Visual: Picture of a raft and team of people working together and going down a swirling cascading river, (PowerPoint® 1). Music: Upbeat, dramatic music (without lyrics) playing reasonably loudly as the rest of the team come in.
Who will introduce you? How will they do this?	CFO — A key ally in this project — enormous credibility with audience.
How will you connect with the audience?	I will ask a provocative question to link the slide and the music to the message. Then I will allow 5 minutes for discussion. E.g. "Did you have a good night's sleep last night? Great, because once I tell you about the challenges we face as a team, you might not sleep so well tonight! Fortunately for us, we are all in this together. We, as a team, hold the solution to the greatest challenge of our careers." Discuss the difference between working alone and working as a team.
How will you call them to action? (In a sentence)	I will announce, "At the end of this presentation I will be asking for your personal, active commitment to approve $4 million in capital spending to install a new information system for the whole company."
What is your benefit statement?	"Each person here today has extensive business experience and the ability to make smart business decisions. However, to do so, we need accurate information. As you know, Colossal Sports has lost the $300 million business at 'Marbella Retailers' because we were on stop credit over $200,000 in late payments! (PowerPoint® 2 — picture of retailer). None of us realised. Fortunately, we have a solution, in the form of a new information system that will help you make the right decisions at the right time. As individuals we can look forward to each improving the profits from our respective product lines. As a team, we will amaze the Board with better performance across the whole company."
How will you give the audience a sneak preview of what's to come?	I will say, "During the next 2 hours together I would like to show you a short video on the next generation information system and to discuss how implementing a new information system will benefit all of us. Let's put our heads together and come up with an action plan for the new system."

THE OPENING TOOL: COMMUNITY GARDEN

Presentation title	Why the community needs a community garden
Duration	10 minutes
How will you 'set the scene' for the audience arrival? (Music, picture, beverages available, meet and greet.)	On arrival an abundant platter of organic food will appear and be offered to the councillors. This fruit and vegetables will be grown from another neighbouring community garden.
Who will introduce you? How will they do this?	Minister for Sustainability, Environment, Water, Population and Communities, The Hon Tony Burke MP. He will briefly introduce our project and reinforce his support.
How will you connect with the audience?	I will bring out a bag of store-bought groceries filled with similar produce to what they have just been enjoying. I will do a price and quality comparison.
How will you call them to action? (In a sentence)	I will announce, "At the end of this presentation I will be asking for council support and $10,000 funding toward the garden and allocating the plot of land for the betterment and enjoyment of the local community."
What is your benefit statement?	"To begin with I will outline relevant statistics of the increase in disconnected communities as well as the increase of food costs. The images I will be showing will be Aerial shots of the local area and the inability for high rise tenants to grow anything. The solution is to create an area for people to grow their own vegetables and fruit which will help increase council's popularity and community spirit."
How will you give the audience a sneak preview of what's to come?	Announce, "Over the next 40 minutes I will look at the community needs, explain how other community gardens work and outline all of the key supporters of this community garden. I will then also address costs, possible locations and what will be involved."

Insight 17
Structure Your Content

*"Life is about choices. And choices have consequences.
Even a non-decision is a choice and it has consequences."*

Judy Mullins — IBM

In earlier insights we recommended when you start writing your presentation, you should start with the close because it helps focus your attention on the outcome you want. When you move on to the content stage, you will be more ruthless with what you present and more importantly what you leave out. You have a clear idea about how you will finish and what you want the audience to do next.

Relate to real things in your structure

Try to make your facts connect with your audience. Statistics are often dry and are hard to absorb and may need a real-life reference point. For example, we recently listened to a friend telling his son about the size of a humpback whale. Kilograms and tonnes were lost on the eight year old, as they might be on an adult. The exasperated father finally barked, "It is about the size of eleven elephants!" The child became wide eyed and shrieked with astonishment, suddenly realising the enormity of the whale.

While units of measurement were boring and meaningless to the boy, he could imagine eleven elephants. So, when you are relaying a fact to your audience, try to put it in terms that they will relate to and understand.

As well as making statistics relevant, avoid generalisations. Be specific in what you say. Your facts will sound more credible if you give exact figures rather than saying "most people". So, instead of saying, "Whales are **really** big!" you might like to say, "A humpback whale weighs over 37,000 kilograms—that is the size of eleven elephants." Adding a picture of a set of scales with the whale on one side and eleven elephants on the other side would be even more powerful.

Specify Actions

You need to specify the action you want your audience to take, and the benefits of the action. For example, instead of saying, "You should exercise more to get fit", say, "You should exercise for forty minutes, three times a week and you will see your body shape begin to change after three weeks". The second statement is more inspiring, because people can see what they have to do to achieve a specific goal.

Your Main Points

It is one thing to do your research, but it is another to make sure it is clearly presented. People retain information better if a general structure is given first and the details are filled in later. Remember, your entire presentation should be broken down into between three and seven points.

After you complete your research, it will become a question of what to leave out rather than what to put in. The audience will want evidence of your statements, but they do not need to be bombarded with information. Be careful of 'information overload'. When deciding what evidence to include: be ruthless.

As discussed in *Insight 7—The Presentation Preparation Process*, you need to choose how many main points to include in your presentation.

The table below from *Insight 7* summarises our advice.

NUMBER OF MAIN IDEAS	COMMENTS
3	Will make complex information simpler. Takes significant time and effort. Aids persuasion.
4	Often can be represented in a box with quarters (a 2 by 2 matrix or box). A 2 by 2 box is an efficient way of presenting information and helps make the message more memorable.
5	Recommended for most presentations as a trade-off between clarity, time and resources.
7	Maximum to allow people to remember the structure. The audience may not act because they do not remember or understand. This is the fastest to create.

Once you have identified your main points, use this as a framework. Allocate each point a certain time slot within the presentation, then go through and add detail to each point. This will ensure that each point is covered adequately and appropriately. This is the time to use statistics, quotes, stories, and any other evidence that support your points.

A good way to do this is by using a content model that will be explained in more detail in *Insight 18—Choose a Content Model*. Models are useful because they:

- Structure your presentation.
- Improve the flow of your message.
- Prepare the audience to take action.

Choose a model from the options outlined in *Insight 18* and then arrange your content according to that model.

Choosing a content model

You can structure your content in two ways:

- Sequence your actions.
- Sequence your ideas.

These options can then be broken down into the categories seen in the following tree.

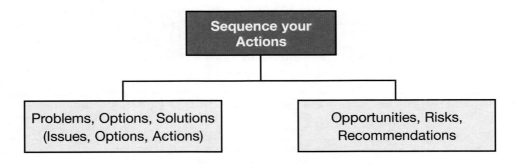

These options will be explored in the following Insight.

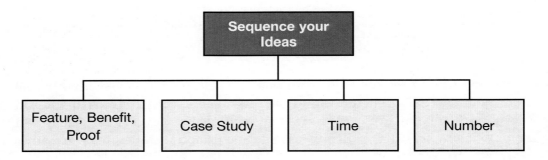

Insight 18
Choose a Content Model

"It is a bit like being a mosquito in a nudist camp. You know what you have to do, but you don't know where to start."

Unknown

| Understand Audience | Research Data | Write Close | Write Opening | **Structure Content** |

Content Models

When structuring the content of your presentation, content models are extremely effective. Not only do content models save time, but they help your audience remember, by avoiding information overload. Another benefit is content models help the presenter steer your audience towards the action you want.

As we discussed in *Insight 17—Structure Your Content*, there are two kinds of content models—those based on actions and those based on ideas. When Persuading for Results, you want the audience to take action, so we recommend you try to use a content model based on action. An action model frames the presentation so, at the end of the presentation the audience unconsciously expects to be told what action they should take.

Contrast this with a content model based on ideas, which often leads to an information dump. The risk is, at the end of the presentation the audience will focus on the ideas and will not expect to be told to take action.

However, content models for ideas can be useful in two ways. First you can use them to sequence evidence and sub-points within your main points, organised by action. Second, if you are in a hurry, use them because they are quick to apply. After all, any model is better than a meandering mix of points.

Sequence Your Actions

Problems, Options, Solutions

Everyone has problems of one kind or another and most people want to solve their problems. With this model, you identify problems, present some options for solving the problems and recommend a particular solution. This model can be very effective, but there are some hazards when identifying problems.

First, sometimes people do not like to be reminded about problems. So, it might be more appropriate to frame the presentation using more neutral terms, such as 'Issues, Options and Recommendations'.

Second, the audience will usually only take action when a problem is urgent or serious or better still, both urgent and serious. Neil Rackham studied sales people, who depend on identifying problems and persuading people to take action. In *The Spin Selling Fieldbook*, he explains that after identifying a problem, the most effective persuaders:

- Investigated implications and consequences of the problem; and
- Explored benefits and consequences of solving the problem.

You need to explore the implications of a problem before the audience will understand why it is serious and urgent. For each problem ask:

- What are the implications of the problem?
- What is affected by the problem?
- Who is affected by the problem?
- What are the consequences of the problem?

After all, the more serious and more urgent you can show the problems are, the more likely the audience will take action. Ensure you spend plenty of time during your preparation and presentation for demonstrating the seriousness and urgency of the problems.

Once you have showed the seriousness and urgency of the problem, explore the solution:

- What is the best solution?
- What are the benefits of the solution?

- What are the consequences of the solution?
- What are the consequences of doing nothing?

In every situation there is the option of doing nothing and as many experienced persuaders will tell you, this is a popular choice. Therefore, you should always ask the audience about the consequences of doing nothing. If there are no serious or urgent consequences, then do not be surprised if the audience members do not take action!

Opportunity, Risks, Recommendation

Business leaders constantly face opportunities that have risks. When asking people to take action that involves risk, it is better to acknowledge the risks than to ignore them. After all, ignoring the risks during your presentation does not guarantee the audience has not thought of them.

You might say, "We have a great opportunity before us. The risks we face with this opportunity are 1, 2, and 3. There are three courses of action available to us. These are A, B, and C. Based on our analysis our best option is A, because this option allows us to minimise the risk in the following way…"

Where there is risk, it is always best to acknowledge it. Identify the risks and discuss their severity and probability. If you ignore the risks, you will lose credibility because the audience might think you have overlooked vital information. In *Insight 22—Visuals Add Value*, we show a useful technique for displaying risks.

As we discussed in *Insight 4—Choosing Winning Frames*, sometimes a useful frame for risk and uncertainty is Real Options. The two ideas of Real Options are to create options that have a much higher upside than downside and to have a portfolio of options, monitor the uncertainty and exercise only those options that are 'in the money'. This approach contrasts with the 'big bet' approach where a business gambles everything on their best judgement or best guess.

Sequence Your Ideas

Feature, Benefit, Proof

If you are called to present to a prospective client, or to showcase your products, the 'Feature, Benefit, Proof' model is a well-tested approach.

Outlining features and benefits is relatively simple. For example, if you are selling a photocopier, you might sell the features by saying "This photocopier has twenty sorting trays and puts through forty pages a minute. You will save time collating and printing. This means that your staff can be assigned to other tasks."

But what about proof? Consider how much more successful you will be at persuading people to part with their money if you can prove that they will reap the promised benefits. Vague hearsay evidence is not sufficient. Instead of saying "eight out of ten people say…" cite evidence such as, "Studies at XYZ University in 2010 showed conclusively that…" Better still, prove the benefits through hands on experience. For example, you could offer the photocopier to the company for one month free of charge. At the end of the month, they have the opportunity to purchase the copier if they believe they have received the promised benefit.

When using this model, be sure that you pace your presentation to suit the audience, and that you add zest to the message. If you do not, you can fall into the trap of just making a 'sales pitch'.

Case Study

Most people are familiar with the use of case studies. It is as simple as finding examples to support your message. You may draw upon examples from your experience, the industry of the audience, from popular culture or from the news. Ideally, they should feel it could be them or to one of their colleagues that you are talking about.

A real case study will breathe life into your message. A few months after the presentation people may have forgotten the details of the presentation, but might be able to recall an interesting case study.

Case studies also tap into people's emotions. This is powerful because humans are emotional beings and seldom make purely rational decisions. Psychologists have researched decision-making processes and have discovered that logic often plays only a small part in the outcome. Therefore, you can increase the persuasive force of your message by framing it in a case study that your audience can relate to.

We suggest the following ways to use case studies:

- Give an example of a person faced with a situation relevant to your message.
- Give a set of circumstances and point out the available choices.
- Give the examples of the consequences of decisions.

For example, a human resources manager might want the company to adopt a team-based approach. He or she might say, "Six months ago we switched from an individual to a team sales approach and since then sales have increased by 15%. The evidence for this is in the graph that I distributed. A survey last month showed that customer satisfaction has risen dramatically since the change, as has staff morale. I think we could implement the team-based model throughout the company with similar improvements. I would now like to outline the way the teams function and offer examples of how the team model can be implemented in your division of the company."

Time: Past, Present and Future

This model is particularly powerful when you are trying to appeal to the emotional side of your audience. If your presentation is designed to motivate people who face a common situation, this approach may be best.

This model works logically through a sequence of events. A classic example of this approach was President John F. Kennedy's reaction to Russia's progress in the 1950s space race. John F. Kennedy made impassioned presentations that consisted of three main points. They were:

- This is what we have been doing in the past—giving examples of America's efforts to put men in space.
- This is what is happening now—the Russians are moving ahead.
- This is what needs to happen in the future—we must be the premier nation in space. In ten years we will have put a man on the moon.

Number

The Number Model is useful if you have a short time to prepare your presentation because it is the simplest content model to use. It works well with all audience members. Simply list the main points as 1, 2, 3 and so on. List subordinate points as 1a, 1b, 2a, or 2(a)i, 2(a)ii, or 1.1, 1.2 and so on.

You might introduce your structure by saying, "I have three points to discuss about this new research. The first is about where the research was conducted. The second point is about how the research was conducted. The third is about the outcome of the research. Let me start with the first point. The research was conducted at..."

Which model to use?

CONTENT MODEL	BENEFITS	BEST USED WHEN
Problems, Options, Solutions **(Issues, Options, Actions)**	Effective to encourage action if the audience sees there is a serious or urgent problem. (A more positive frame that avoids the negative connotations of 'problems'.)	Problems are serious or urgent or both. (The audience caused some of the problems or there are high emotions in the audience.)
Opportunities, Risks, Recommendations	A positive model, focusing on the future. It acknowledges risks.	A decision needs to be made, but there is an element of risk.
Feature, Benefit, Proof	Allows the features of a product/service/plan or strategy to be showcased to audience. Appeals to logic.	Trying to sell a product, service or idea. Trying to implement a new plan or strategy.
Case Study	Draws on lessons from others. Appeals to emotions.	Motivating an audience. Showing benefits of certain behaviours, attitudes or processes. There is parallel between your topic and an example.
Time: Past, Present, Future	Allows audience to see how your idea/plan fits into the sequence of events. Appeals to emotions.	Trying to motivate the audience. Proposing a new plan or idea that follows on or has developed from an old one. There is a clear sequence of events.
Number	Easy to prepare. Simple structure. Appeals to logic.	There are a few definite points to cover. The main points are fairly independent of each other. There is little time to prepare.

The Content Tool

THE CONTENT TOOL: COLOSSAL SPORTS		
Duration	3hrs & 10 mins	
What is your main objective?	To persuade the audience the new system will greatly improve the way they do business, and it is the best system available for the job.	
What action do you want the audience to take?	I want them to approve the system and commit to it financially.	
What content model will you use?	Time: Past, Present, Future	

KEY POINTS	TIMING	RESOURCES
PAST		
Rapid growth of total business and profitability for each year.	30 mins	PowerPoint® 3.
When the company broke into 3 business groups.		Video 1.
Impact on the financial viability of the business.		
The new information system installed.		PowerPoint® 4.
Review expenditure and the return of investment.		PowerPoint® 5.
Picture of founder and share price, indicating that she made all the earlier decisions.		PowerPoint® 6.
Q & A	15 min	
Three business groups with various growth patterns and profitability.	20 mins	PowerPoint® 7, 8, 9 & 10.
How poor decisions are made in the absence of timely information — video address from the Chairman of 'Marbella Retailers'.		Video 2.
Open discussion on 'do we want growth or stability?'		PowerPoint® 11.
Q & A	30 mins	

FUTURE		
Overview of the new information system and application to the whole business.	40 mins	PowerPoint® 12 & 13.
Implications for the three business groups.		PowerPoint® 14, 15 & 16.
Compared to existing system and the benefits to approving $4 million IT changes.		PowerPoint® 17.
Impact if decision is not made.		PowerPoint® 18.
Future impact on growth if the decision is positive.		PowerPoint® 19.
FINAL Q & A	55 mins	

THE CONTENT TOOL: COMMUNITY GARDEN

Duration	1 hour
What is your main objective?	To gain approval and support to instigate a sustainable, community garden.
What action do you want the audience to take?	Give permission to start planning Allocate a site Allocate $10,000 funding
What content model will you use?	Problems, Options, Solutions

KEY POINTS	TIMING	RESOURCES
PROBLEMS		
Diminished community Spirit	10 mins	Slide of discontented people in over-developed community
Increased living cost (especially the cost of organic food)		Comparative cost and examples of fresh produce grown from community garden compared to equivalent store-bought groceries
Increased levels of waste		Slide with photo of overflowing waste and statistics of food scraps wasted each year
Increased need for public recreation spaces due to increased population		Slide — picture of over-crowded local public spaces
OPTIONS		
1. Do nothing = unhappy people	10 mins	
2. Reduce development in the area = unlikely		
3. Create a community garden = happy healthy community who produce less waste		Slide of happy group of diverse people in a community garden

SOLUTIONS		
Allocate a plot for a community Garden	20 mins	Aerial shots and photos of some proposed sites
Support the project by allocation $10,000 to the set up of the project		Funding plan in the handout
Detailed plan of how it will work and be sustainable		Plan for memberships, fund raiser activities, seed sowing and maintenance
Create a large compost / worm farm to turn organic waste into a resource to use on the garden		Brochures of the available large compost & worm farm options/solutions
Use the community garden as an education centre for organic gardening and healthy living / eating		

Insight 19
Using Notes

"A short pencil is far better than a long memory."

Usually, you can use visuals in your presentation. Mostly, these can be used as a prompt to remind you of points you need to cover. However, occasionally visual aids are not available and you must rely on your memory or use notes.

Sometimes the wording is critical because there are legal requirements such as a listed company presenting financial statements to groups of analysts or investors. Sometimes the stakes are high for example a company defending a merger proposal. In these situations you will often have a complete script.

Effective Notes

In most situations, you will make do with brief notes in point form. You might prefer to have the main points as headings, each on their own card, with a few words underneath to remind you of facts or anecdotes you wanted to share.

If you reduce your presentation to short points, rather than writing out the entire speech, then you will present it naturally in more of a conversational tone. An audience appreciates a presentation that is planned, but allows for spontaneity. Point form also allows you to skip less important information if you are running out of time.

We recommend that you practice your presentations standing up, and record your practice on audio or video tape. This allows you to listen to the tape, check timing and to hear any problems in the delivery and order of your points. This practice will help you polish the presentation and will also increase your confidence.

When reading a script is necessary

However, if you do need to read your presentation, here are a few tips:

- Type the presentation in a large font, with black ink. It should be double or triple spaced, but not so widely spaced that you need to turn the page every few sentences.
- Include signals for pause and emphasis in the script.
- Number each page and staple your presentation. If you drop your notes, you can pick them up and continue.
- Check that every page is there and that you have a spare copy of the presentation.
- Practice the script several times and tape the practices. Review the tape particularly for timing and emphasis of words.

Reasons not to read

There are at least five compelling reasons not to 'read' your presentation.

1. You will lose eye contact with your audience.
2. You may lose rapport with your audience.
3. Your voice may become monotonous.
4. You could fail to notice that your audience has become bored or confused.
5. You may find it hard to weave your way back into the script, if you have to stop to answer a question.

We can all train ourselves to speak without having to read a presentation word for word. After all, we do it every day in a thousand situations. All you need to do is to transfer the skills you use in a one-to-one conversation to your group delivery.

Be natural

The key to being natural is to know your material. The confidence that comes from comprehensive knowledge of your subject will enable you to speak authoritatively without needing a written presentation. You will not need a prepared presentation if you relate your points to insights or experiences that are familiar to you and the audience—you can 'talk' to them in a much more natural way.

When to Think on Your Feet®!

Sometimes you simply do not have time to prepare. Take, for example, the crucial Q&A session after your presentation. You literally have to 'think on your feet'. The best tools we have seen for these situations are found in the globally available workshop Think On Your Feet®. See www.thinkonyourfeet.com for details.

The 'secret' to the Think on Your Feet® approach involves 'recipes for reasoning'. These free you to organise your ideas 'on the spot'. The results are clear, brief, memorable answers—and more credibility for you. If your role involves thinking quickly and delivering quickly, then attending one of these workshops will give you great value.

Insight 20
Question Time

*"Any Questions?
I've got an answer and I'd like to use it."*

Rodney Marks — Humorist

If you are presenting to a small group you may encourage the audience to ask questions as you go along. For a larger group, it is probably best if you allocate a set time towards the end of your presentation to answer any questions.

Presenters often dread question time. It is the unpredictable part of the presentation. You cannot control what people might ask. What if the audience voices its scepticism? What if the questions are very technical? What if...? What if...? What if...?

Enjoy Questions

There is no reason to be intimidated by question time. People who ask questions are usually just interested in your message. Seize the opportunity to clarify any details and to reinforce your main points. By taking questions, you are able to clear up misconceptions and make the presentation especially relevant to the audience.

Planning for Question Time

The best way to plan for question time is to have two or three questions prepared in advance. Anticipate questions the audience might ask. There are two ways to do this:

1. Read through your material thoroughly and note any possible questions.
2. Rehearse your presentation with a friend or colleague and ask them to raise questions.

The result of pre-empting your audience's questions will be two-fold. First, you will have well prepared answers, which will increase your credibility as a presenter. Second, you will be more relaxed and comfortable in the period leading up to question time.

Opening Question Time

Before inviting questions from the audience, you might say, "We have covered a lot of points. Let me pose a couple of questions to you..." This is an effective way to get everyone thinking.

Then throw the ball over to the audience. Let them know how long you intend to take questions for and monitor the time. For instance, you could say, "We have ten minutes now for questions. Who would like to ask the first?"

Answering Questions

A great way to acknowledge a question is to respond with, "That is a very good question" or "Your question raises an interesting point." Even a simple, "Thanks for the question", helps to build rapport with the audience.

Once you have acknowledged the question, it is important to repeat the question back to the audience to ensure that everyone has heard it. Rephrasing the question into your own words gives you an opportunity to make sure you have interpreted the question correctly and gives you a moment to consider your response.

It is important to respond to the individual who posed the question. However, seek eye contact with people in different parts of the audience, so everyone is engaged and involved in the answer.

Keeping the questions moving is an art in itself. When time is of the essence, we suggest that you do not return to the person who asked you the question. You do not want to get bogged down in a conversation that may not be beneficial for the rest of the audience.

The Loaded Question

We admit that managing question time can sometimes be difficult. You might come across someone in the audience who will use the opportunity to undermine your credibility or berate your ideas. You might be able to spot this person even before the assault begins. It could be the woman slumped down in her seat with her arms folded and eyebrows raised. It might be the man who keeps whispering to his friend. Given half a chance, these people will destroy the hard work that you have done to sell your ideas, your product and your own reputation.

One good way of stealing the thunder of someone who is trying to start an argument is to address their comment in such a way as to leave their negative attitude behind. In response to a hostile question, you might turn back to the audience and repeat the question, say how it relates to your topic and then aim your response at the whole audience. This takes the momentum away from the person who originally asked the question. React to the question, not to the emotion or acrimony behind it and do not get drawn into an argument with audience members. You should refer to *Insight 39—Managing Problem Participants*, for more information on dealing with difficult people during question time.

You do not have to have an answer

If you do not know an answer, confidently remark that you want to give an accurate and comprehensive answer, and therefore, you will postpone answering the question until later. Make a note of it and make sure you do get around to it. Ask the questioner for a business card so you have their contact details.

Alternatively, toss the question out to the group and see if anyone else wishes to suggest an answer. No one will expect you to know everything, and they will respect your honesty when you say, "Actually, that is not an area that I am an expert in. Leave it with me and I will get back to you." Or, if you know of someone who could provide a better explanation, suggest they contact this person.

If the question is irrelevant to your topic, respond by letting the questioner know that it is a separate issue which you do not have time to go into. Say something like, "That is a good point, but it doesn't really relate to today's topic, so I will leave it for now."

Ending Question Time

Forewarn your audience that question time will be drawing to an end. Say something like, "We have time for two more questions, who has the first one?"

Where possible, it is a good idea to remain for a period after the presentation to discuss any further questions. Some audience members may not want to ask their question in front of the entire audience, because they either lack the confidence or they do not see their question as particularly relevant. It is always encouraging for the audience to see that you are willing to spend your own time discussing their concerns. During question time, if someone is dissatisfied with your answer, let him or her know you will discuss it with them after the presentation.

Remember, in a presentation take the questions and then deliver your close to the presentation. You want people to leave remembering your powerful concluding thoughts rather than any points of contention.

QUESTION TIME TOOL: COLOSSAL SPORTS

How long will you allow for questions?	1hr, 40 mins.
Will you allow questions to be asked as you go or only at the end?	I will allow time at the end of each section for questions.
How will you open the questions? How will you encourage people to talk?	Before I conclude I will ask, "Are there any questions?" or "What are your initial thoughts on the New System?"
What questions do you anticipate the audience will ask?	How much is this going to cost my department?
	Will we have less decision making power, if our every move is scrutinised?
	Who is going to train us in the New System? How long will it take? Will the training costs be coming out of our budget?
	How often do we have to enter data into the New System? How will it impact my day-to-day activities?
	Why is this system better than cheaper systems on the market?
What are your responses to these questions?	Initially each department will have to pay $50,000 to install the software. There will be an estimated $15,000 per annum in maintenance fees. But, this will help reduce the risk of losing another account with $300 million account. In addition, it will give us accurate information to help us achieve our company goal of 15% growth in profits year-on-year for the next five years. With more information, you will actually have more power to influence your bottom line.
	The training will be conducted by our human resources team. Training will only cost you the loss of productivity during the time employees are away from their normal roles.
	Once your staff learns to use the system, there will be minimal data input requirements. This means that they will be more efficient on a day-to-day basis.
	The system is better for Colossal Sports as it was designed specifically to meet our needs (refer back to reasons).
	The changes to our daily routine will give us a fresh start!
How will you respond to irrelevant questions?	"That is an interesting point and perhaps we can look at that at a later date. At the moment we need to focus our thoughts on the New System."

What is your strategy for responding to questions that you do not know the answer to?	Honesty — "I do not know the answer to that. I will find out for you and get back to you via email."
How will you close the question time?	Let them know we are out of time and any further enquiries can be asked later — by phone or email. Then I will conclude.

QUESTION TIME TOOL: COMMUNITY GARDEN

How long will you allow for questions?	5 mins
Will you allow questions to be asked as you go or only at the end?	At the end of the presentation.
How will you open the questions? How will you encourage people to talk?	Are there any questions you would like to ask that you feel have not been covered in my presentation?
What questions do you anticipate the audience will ask?	They may ask about the time-scale of the project How we intend to raise funds from the community? Who will do the maintenance? How will we prevent compost odours?
What are your responses to these questions?	That it will depend on the allocation of land as well as the funding permitted. Remind them of the community support so far & outline ideas for fund raising events held through the churches, schools and local junior soccer club. Direct them to the handouts for detailed proposed maintenance schedules. Show them the brochures for the composting options and give examples of how other community gardens deal with odours. Possibly arrange an inspection of a successful nearby community garden as an example of how it all works in practice.

How will you respond to irrelevant questions?	Acknowledge their question and say that I will discuss it with them personally.
What is your strategy for responding to questions that you do not know the answer to?	Answer honestly, let them know that you will find the answer and get back to them.
How will you close the question time?	Thank you for your questions but our time is up, and I respect that you are all very busy. If there are any more questions, my contact details are on the handout provided.

Insight 21
After the Applause

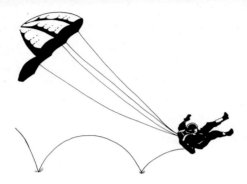

"Training that brings about no change is as useful as a parachute that opens on the second bounce."

Robert W Pike

A presentation that ends without an action plan is a wasted opportunity. The audience should leave understanding what needs to be done, who is responsible for ensuring it gets done, and when the tasks must be completed. The best way to ensure action is taken is to follow up after your presentation.

Summary and Action Plan

A good way to establish contact with the audience after a presentation is to send them a copy of the agreed action. Send it several days after the presentation, to remind them of the action they need to take. Include the main points of the presentation, necessary follow up action, an individualised list of action required from each audience member, and the date and topic of the next presentation.

Depending on how many people attend your presentation, send audience members or key members a follow up that will drive home the point of your presentation. Often this will include a summary of what was discussed at the presentation. This can be done via post or email.

Send a working example

After our presentations, we often send our groups a case study or journal article that emphasises the point we have been talking about. This reminds people of the issues raised in the presentation and allows them to read about a working example. Consider sending a relevant book, a sample of your product, an inspirational poster, or anything else you think will help persuade your audience, or at least the key decision makers.

Call to say thank you

Do not forget to contact the person who was responsible for you giving the presentation in the first place. Make a simple phone call to ask how they thought it went, and whether the presentation covered all the relevant topics. You may like to schedule a meeting to discuss the outcomes in more depth, and suggest other presentations that may assist the targeted audience further. Remember, making an extra effort will distinguish you from other presenters.

Section 3
Style — Powerful Persuaders

"Over the long run, superior performance
depends on superior learning."

Peter Senge

Insight 22
Visuals Add Value

"The soul never thinks without an image."
Aristotle

More than 80% of what we learn is linked to what we see. Research, by the Wharton Applied Research Centre, sponsored by 3M, shows that when a presenter uses visuals, an audience remembers 10% more of the presented information. Also, visuals are processed 60,000 times faster than text. Subsequent research by the University of Minnesota reveals that presenters who use computer-generated visuals are 43% more persuasive than presenters who do not. By using clear and interesting visuals you will hold an audience's interest more easily and you will be perceived as more professional and believable.

We recently worked with a client's team, planning a major new project. The project required capital well above the amount allotted in the budget. We knew that it would be a struggle to get the senior managers to read the report, which contained detailed descriptions of intricate mechanical and process changes. The team had just finished mapping the argument and was starting to create the report. However, the team struggled to find words to describe a particular aspect of the existing production process, and the problems with the current technology.

A client team member said, "I was at a presentation the other day and the presenter showed slides with lots of text. I found myself nodding off to sleep. Then the presenter displayed a slide with a picture. The picture caught my attention and I noticed that other people had started paying attention too."

Together, the team decided to insert pictures into the report. The pictures showed staff experiencing problems with the existing equipment and then showed the new equipment the team wanted to buy. The expenditure was approved and the senior managers remarked "the photographs helped us understand the problems with the existing equipment." A picture can grab your audience's attention and can often be more persuasive than words.

Some extra benefits of visuals are they:

Force order and sequence on the presenter. Sheer nervousness, questions from the audience or other outside factors may interrupt the flow of your presentation. Ordered visuals ensure the sequence of your presentation remains intact.

Require selection of key points. To display visuals effectively you cannot just cram all the information you have into a few slides. Visuals force you to choose simple key points, making the presentation more succinct and focused.

Save time. As the saying goes, "A picture is worth a thousand words". Visual presentations are an effective technique for persuading your audience. Visuals also allow complex ideas to be presented in a simple graphic format that is absorbed more quickly than pure text.

Instil confidence. Visuals can instil confidence in the audience towards the presenter and the message, because the presenter looks more competent and professional.

Choose your Medium

A presenter has many options displaying visuals. These options include samples, posters, props, banners, multimedia productions, videos, slides, whiteboards, flip charts and many others. In product launches, Steve Jobs of Apple makes excellent use of props as he unveils the new iPhone, the MacBook Air or the new iPad. Find the video with Google and watch how he surprises the audience as he unveils the product and the new features.

Consider which visuals will suit your audience. Use flip charts and marker boards for a small, informal audience, as they will encourage audience participation, while larger audiences benefit from visuals.

Here are some ideas for what to include on visuals

- Photographs
- Graphics
- Shapes
- Graphs
- Lists

- Statistics
- Maps
- Cartoons
- Diagrams
- Questions

General Guidelines

When using technology, assume that whatever can go wrong no doubt will. Keep a contact phone number handy for someone who can fix the machine and always have a backup plan. The backup plan for your laptop might be to have your presentation on a USB or handouts of your visuals.

Here are some important points about using visuals effectively:

- Make every visual relevant to the objective of your presentation.
- Colour is more memorable, more dramatic and more fun.
- Keep fonts simple, large and clear and do not use more than two types. Avoid shaded or shadow fonts because they are hard to read.
- The visual standard is one message for each visual, six words per line and six lines per visual.
- Write titles as if they were front-page headlines. Tell your message in a brief and interesting way.

Visuals are great in the opening, content and close phases of your presentation.

Using Diagrams

Sometimes organising content physically works best, either by geography or by a diagram. For example if you were discussing the world market for a product, you could discuss the prospects by regions, such as Asia Pacific, The Americas, Europe, Russia, Africa and the Middle East. Or if discussing a new factory design you might show a drawing of the factory, and then discuss one area at a time. If at the start of each new section, you show the drawing highlighting the next area, the drawing can act as a signpost.

For example we have used a pyramid to show three different kinds of maintenance contracts—a menu contract, an incentive contract and a reliability contract. In a menu contract, a customer directs the contractor to perform an activity from an agreed list of activities each with an agreed cost. In an incentive contract, the contractor can choose to perform activities with the objective of reducing the maintenance cost for the customer. The commercial reward for the contractor is the contractor and the customer share the cost savings. In a reliability contract, the contractor chooses activities to achieve or exceed a given reliability target. Here the customer pays a reward for achieving or exceeding a reliability target.

The complexity of the contract increases as we move up the pyramid. In addition, the trust needed between the contractor and the customer increases as we move up the pyramid. The diagram reinforces this point.

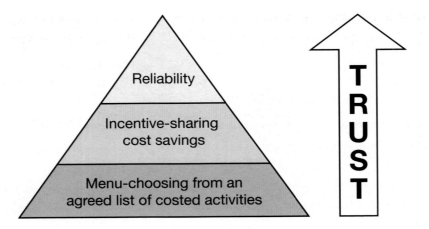

Another diagram that is frequently used is the 2 by 2 matrix. For example, if we were talking about the risks of an opportunity we might use a two by two matrix to organise the discussion on risks. A simple technique of risk analysis is to list the risks, then rate them as high or low on two factors—impact on the business and frequency of occurrence—and plot the risks in one of four quadrants.

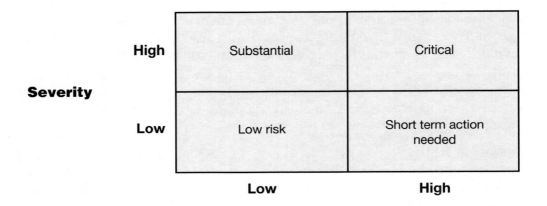

During the introduction, we would show this diagram. Then present in four sections: critical risks, substantial risks, short term actions needed and low risks. Then use the diagram as a signpost, in the corner of a slide and before a section of slides, highlighting the types of risks being discussed.

If you wish to illustrate a process or flow of activities, then a McKinsey value chain is useful. Here you can emphasise different stages with a highlight as you progress through the presentation.

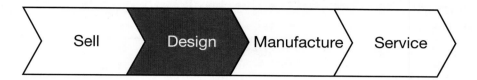

If you use a diagram, remember the principle of keeping your number of main points to seven or less. A complicated diagram can reduce the effectiveness of your persuasion.

VISUALS TOOL: COLOSSAL SPORTS	
Data Projector	Data projector with laptop.
Screen—size/height	2 metres × 2 metres.
Where are the light switches?	Located at the back of the room.
Will the lights be on or off?	On.
What visuals will you use?	Graph of data from the New System to demonstrate what the system can provide for each department. Pictures from Clipart & photographs of rowers.
Background colours/effects	Blue background, flat colour.
Slide Animation	Appear.
Slide Transition	No.
Proof read for typing errors	Will do a final check on Thursday.
What font will you use?	Arial, size 24pt, white on company template.
Will you use bullets?	White arrows.

Here is a Community Garden example of how you could outline the necessary Information.

VISUALS TOOL: COMMUNITY GARDEN	
Data Projector	yes
Screen—size/height	Standard
Where are the light switches?	Next to the door on the left.
Will the lights be on or off?	On
What visuals will you use?	Pictures of community gardens as well as high density unhealthy communities and some bold statistic slides.
Background colours/effects	No
Slide Animation	No
Slide Transition	No
Proof read for typing errors	Ask my friend Rachael Tzatziki to proof read it one week before the presentation.
What font will you use?	Calibri 32
Will you use bullets?	No

Insight 23
Use Visuals for Ideas and Numbers

*"Example is not the main thing in influencing others.
It is the only thing."*

Albert Schweitzer

This section is influenced by one of the world's experts on this topic, Gene Zelazny, Director of Visual Communications for McKinsey and Company. Just pause for a moment and consider that one of the world's top management consultancies pays someone to be a Director of Visual Communications. McKinsey specialises in fact-based analysis, so why pay attention to visual communication? Because, it takes more than logic to persuade an audience to act. The audience must understand, agree and remember. Visuals help people process the message faster and are more persuasive than just words.

Gene Zelazny has more than 40 years of experience designing powerful management reports and presentations. His book, *Say it with Charts: the executive's guide to visual communication* is now in the fourth edition. While we aim to accelerate your learning, we recommend you purchase a copy of Zelazny's book for your library, once you are familiar with the foundations of visual communication outlined here. It is an expensive book, but once you experience how a well-designed visual can help persuade, we think you will agree that it is a wise investment.

We discuss two kinds of visuals, one for ideas and one for numbers. Visuals for ideas seem to be the least understood, so we will begin there. We begin with an example from outside business. One of the authors has helped Results Australia, an organisation of volunteers who lobby governments to increase aid for poor people around the world (www.results.org.au). The importance of overseas aid is often difficult to understand and communicate. Most of the information comes from government organisations and the writing style is 'heavy'. Read the following text and rate it on a scale of 1 to 10, where

1 means you do not understand the material and do not understand what is the problem.

10 means you understand the material and understand the problem.

Then look at the diagrams and rate them in the same way.

The Diseases of Poverty

The World Health Organisation (WHO) indicates that infectious diseases are responsible for almost half of mortality in developing countries. These deaths occur primarily among the poorest people because they do not have access to the drugs and treatment necessary for prevention or cure.

The WHO also indicates that approximately half of infectious disease mortality can be attributed to just three diseases — HIV, Tuberculosis (TB) and Malaria — the diseases of poverty. These three diseases cause over 300 million illnesses and more than 7 million deaths each year.

In addition to suffering and death, these diseases penalise poor communities, as they perpetuate poverty through work loss, school drop-out, decreased financial investment and increased social instability. For example, Africa's combined GDP would be up to $100 billion greater if malaria had been eliminated. Similarly, a nation can expect a decline in GDP of approximately 1% per year when more than 20% of the adult population is infected with HIV.

Treatment and its availability

The drugs to treat TB cost just $US10 for a full six-month course. However, only one quarter of those with active TB have access to effective treatment.

The great majority of malaria deaths could be prevented with drugs costing a few cents. Also insecticide-treated bed-nets cost around $US4 and can help prevent infection.

In 2001, retroviral treatment reached a mere 30,000 Africans with AIDS. A staggering 2,200,000 were doomed to die earlier than necessary.

The Global Fund to Fight AIDS, Tuberculosis and Malaria

The 'Global Fund' was created to assist developing countries to increase resources for the prevention, treatment, care and support of people living with and affected by HIV, TB and malaria. World leaders at the United Nations General Assembly Special Session on HIV unanimously endorsed it in June 2001. The Fund came into operation in January 2002, to attract, manage and disburse additional resources from governments, foundations, the private sector and wealthy individuals, to tackle these three diseases.

To substantially reduce the incidence of all three diseases would require total annual funding from all sources of between $US 9 billion and $US 12 billion, including between $US 7 billion and $US 10 billion to combat AIDS and $US 2 billion to combat TB and malaria.

Australia's Commitment

Health assistance is a significant component of Australia's overseas aid, estimated at $225 million (13% of total overseas aid) in 2003–04. As part of a recent six-year and $200 million HIV initiative, spending in 2003–04 was $60 million. Aid to address other infectious diseases will be 7% of total health aid (about $16 million).

However, Australia was one of the few donor countries yet to contribute to the Global Fund, citing its perceived lack of focus on the Asia-Pacific region and thus adopting a 'wait and see' approach. This was despite the evidence that showed that in its first two years of grants, the Global Fund committed 21% (approx. $478 million) of its funds to South-East Asia and the Pacific. This was more than double the Australian Government's total overseas aid budget for HIV over six years. The Global Fund is therefore able to provide a scale of assistance way beyond the capacity of any single government's overseas aid program.

Your rating out of 10:

Now compare those thoughts and look at the diagrams:

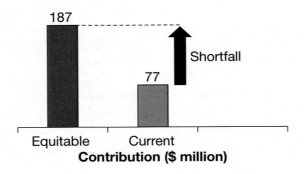

Australia falls short of an equitable contribution to curing the 3 Diseases of poverty

187

77

Shortfall

Equitable   Current

Contribution ($ million)

Your rating out of 10:

When most people read the text, their eyes glaze over because there are so many terms and numbers. In contrast, the diagrams highlight the two issues clearly and quickly:

When we see a gap between where something is and where it should be, our brain asks two questions: "How can we close the gap and why should we close the gap?" Your job, Persuading for Results, is to raise awareness of gaps and recommend ways of closing them. Visuals are very powerful tools for this task.

Gene Zelazny devotes a section of his book to presenting ideas, and looks at how to show interaction, leverage, obstacles, structure, sequence and process. Here are some examples:

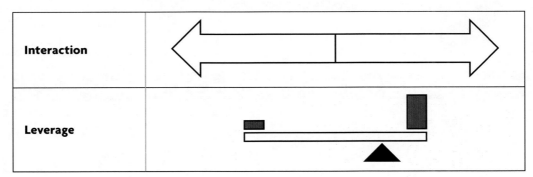

| **Interaction** | |
| **Leverage** | |

Forces	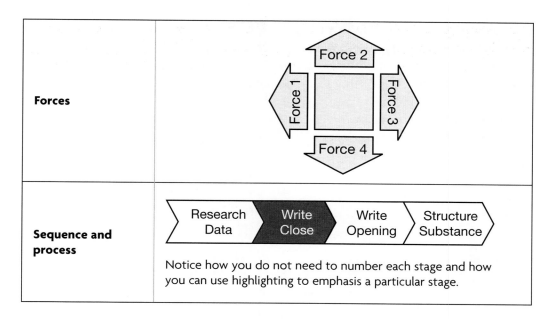
Sequence and process	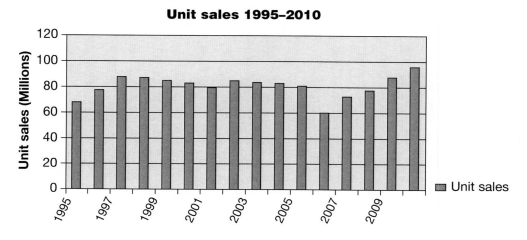Notice how you do not need to number each stage and how you can use highlighting to emphasis a particular stage.

A good tool for creating these diagrams is Microsoft Visio. Visio is not an easy program to use at first. However it is worth persevering with because it has a good selection of ready-made diagrams and is very powerful for creating your own diagrams. We have found the book *Visio for Dummies* by Walkowski helpful. We recommend you only use Visio if everyone on the team has it as it is difficult to change things without the software.

We now move on to discuss charts for numbers. Again we will begin with an example. Many people will create their charts from Microsoft packages. Let us assume we are trying to decide whether to increase capacity to produce a product. So, we create a chart showing the trend in unit sales from 1995–2010. This is how it might appear from a Microsoft package:

Our first question is what is the message of the chart? Is the message that sales have averaged approximately 80 million units? Or is the message that there was a dip in sales in 2006 and sales are now growing? There are several conclusions that can be drawn from the chart, meaning that the presenter will have difficulty guiding the audience's interpretation. Instead, we need to decide what the message is, but first let's simplify the existing chart. We delete 'chartjunk' by simplifying the axes by reducing the number of labels, deleting gridlines, borders and fills. This produces a clearer chart.

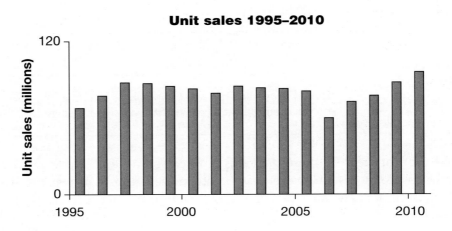

Now let's assume we want to look at the long-term average to see what might be the right production capacity. The message we want to show is that the long term average sales are 81 million. Two ways to present the chart are:

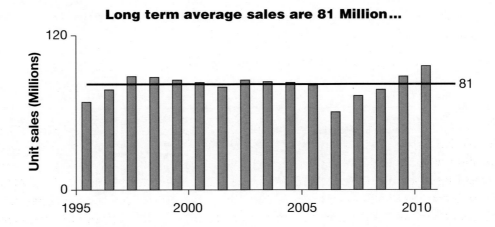

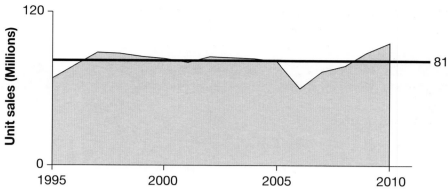

Notice how the message is in the title to ensure the reader gets the intended message. Also, notice the colour has been removed from the bars to increase the focus on the average. The chart now delivers the message clearly. However, because we have made the chart clearer, some of the audience might ask "is there a trend showing increasing sales and therefore does the business need extra capacity above 81 million units?" In anticipation of this question we have prepared another slide.

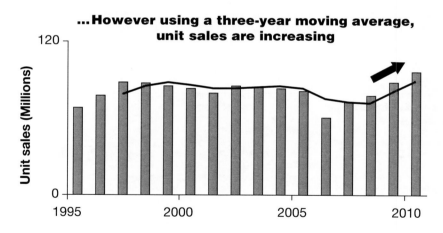

Notice how we put the new message in the title and also add an arrow for emphasis. The golden rule is only one message for each visual. Some presenters argue that one slide with several messages is acceptable. However it takes longer to present several messages in one slide than to explain each one with a separate slide. Also, the audience has to work harder to understand a slide with more than one message. The easier we make it for the audience to understand and remember the message, the more likely they are to be persuaded to act.

Next, we consider how to choose the right chart. This following table is adapted from Mary Munter, who summarises the work of Gene Zelazny in her excellent **Guide to Managerial Communication** which is now in its eighth edition.

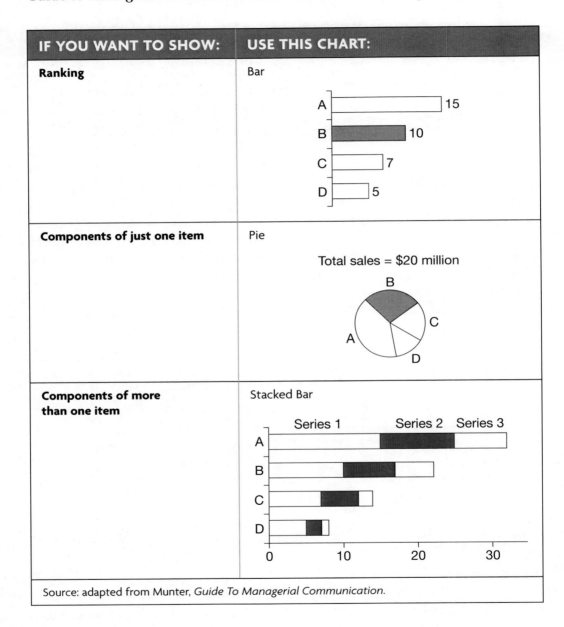

IF YOU WANT TO SHOW:	USE THIS CHART:
Ranking	Bar
Components of just one item	Pie
Components of more than one item	Stacked Bar

Source: adapted from Munter, *Guide To Managerial Communication*.

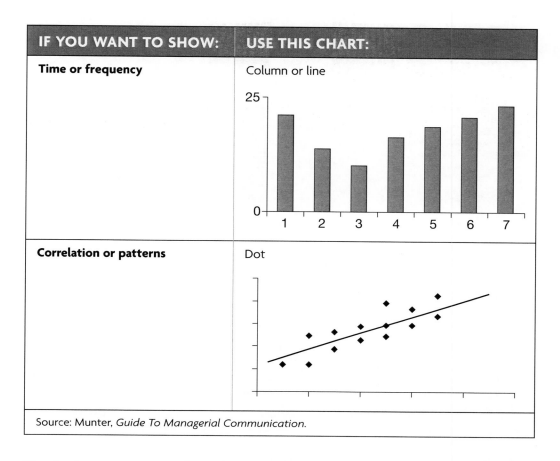

IF YOU WANT TO SHOW:	USE THIS CHART:
Time or frequency	Column or line
Correlation or patterns	Dot

Source: Munter, *Guide To Managerial Communication.*

The final message comes from the experience of Gene Zelazny. How often should we use particular charts? He suggests that we need to use more bar charts and fewer pie charts. In many business situations, we examine market share, however we are really interested in how big our share is **compared** to our competitors. In other words we want to know how we **rank** compared to our competition. So, many of the pie charts we use would be more effective as bar charts. The chart below shows how often people use each kind of chart.

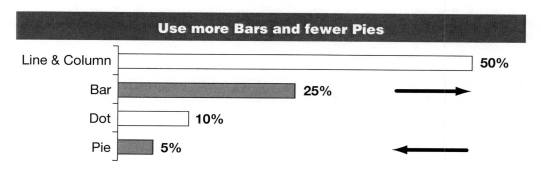

Use more Bars and fewer Pies

Line & Column — 50%
Bar — 25%
Dot — 10%
Pie — 5%

Insight 24
Colour

"Everything is connected to everything else."

Leonardo da Vinci

Colour is a powerful tool that can enhance any presentation. Research shows that colours can evoke an emotional response and make your message more memorable and persuasive. However the psychological impact of colour can also ruin your persuasive message, so think carefully about your choice of colour.

A simple but effective technique to make a presentation to a company more persuasive is to use the colours they use in their branding or in their in-house presentations. This makes your message more persuasive because it seems to fit with how they do business and improves your rapport with them. But when matching colours make sure you use the correct colours. A simple and free tool that will save you hours when matching colours is called instant eyedropper http://instant-eyedropper.com.

In this Insight, we recommend various other ways of incorporating colour into your presentations and we also explain the reasons behind our recommendations, based on the emotion and logic of colour.

But first, let's look at one of our experiences with colour.

We recently worked with a group who were about to persuade a highly successful Asia-Pacific business director to enter a (potentially lucrative) business partnership. The presenters needed to persuade this director that their company was innovative and visionary. The message was good and the content model was fantastic. However, we were stunned to see that the presenters had chosen a murky light brown background for the presentation. On the small screen, the brown colours looked quite distinguished with subtle gradients and background effects. However, with a data projector on a larger screen, the detail was lost and the presentation simply looked boring, bland and negative.

With only a few minutes until 'showtime' we changed the background to a light blue, changed the headings to a bold, clear font and inserted uplifting, colourful photographs. The presenters then made a successful pitch to a director, who remarked that the company seemed to have 'a level of energy and vitality that bodes well for the future.' We doubt he would have responded this way to a murky brown presentation. Remember, what looks good on a small screen does not always look good when projected onto a big screen.

Beginning with our recommendations, we suggest that presenters:

- Use more black.
- Try for a twosome or a trio of colour.
- Choose culturally appropriate colours.

Use more black

Having suggested that colour is important, we begin our discussion with black. The use of black is more powerful than people recognise and the techniques surrounding the use of black have implications for the use of other colours.

As a starting point, we suggest that you design a visual that is effective in black and white, before adding colour. If the visual makes a big impact in black and white, then it will be even better with a splash of colour. In contrast, a rainbow of colours tends to emphasise nothing in particular.

When using black, it is useful to introduce variety through shading. Our design standard incorporates four shades: 0%, 25%, 75% and 100%. Two of these need bold black text and two need bold white text. Adding one other design element, using a 50% shade for the lines instead of black, produces a simple and powerful design standard. The table below shows the combinations and the contrast with a 50% shaded line.

Bold Black Text on 0% shade
Bold Black Text on 25% shade
Bold White Text on 75% shade
Bold White Text on 100% shade

As usual, the best way to learn about colour is to experiment. Try using 50% shading for the lines in your tables instead of 100% black. Use some white text on 100% black. If you are interested in the elements of graphic design, Roger Parker explains these well in his book *Looking Good in Print*.

Try for a Twosome or a Trio

With colour, the key is sparing, well-considered use. We recommend using three colours or less on a visual. While colour provides opportunities for creativity, colour should be used to enhance your message, not simply to decorate it.

The default on most programs that create charts—Excel®, PowerPoint® and Visio®—will produce charts with a rainbow of colours. However, fewer colours are usually more effective. The most effective number of colours, judging from world flags, seems to be three. Remember, a rainbow of colours emphasises nothing.

Choose Colours for the Culture

As we will discuss below, the emotions triggered by various colours are culturally specific. In this sense, culture could refer to the culture of a country, an industry, a firm or even a department.

Barbara Munter, in *Guide To Managerial Communication*, explains that death is symbolised by black in most Western cultures, white in many Eastern cultures, yellow in many Muslim cultures and purple in parts of South America. Choosing the colour might mean the death of your persuasion.

Similarly, using the theme colours of your audience's rival may create the impression that you are not trustworthy, or that you don't understand their business. For example, it would be ill-advised to base a presentation to Pepsi on a red and white colour theme.

The Emotion and Logic Of Colour

Having made our recommendations we will now examine some of the reasons for our recommendations. One of the themes in this book is that persuasion needs both emotion and logic, to influence the heart and the head. Therefore, we must investigate the emotional and logical impact of colour.

The Emotions of Colour

As we have mentioned, the emotions triggered by colour are culturally specific. For example, in the West, red stands for danger, whereas in China it represents joy. Some of the possible images linked to colour are given in the following table.

COLOURS HAVE DIFFERENT MEANINGS	
Colour	Some Meanings
Red	Fire, danger, passion, love, blood, stop, heat, hell, Christmas.
Orange	Autumn, sunrise, sunset.
Yellow	Sunlight, cowardice, joy, summer.
Green	Nature, jealousy, illness, Christmas, money.
Blue	Water, sky, ice, cold, sadness, calm.
Purple	Grapes, depression, frustration, feminism, royalty.
White	Snow, purity, weddings, doves, surrender, peace, angels, heaven.
Black	Night, death, evil, magic, loneliness, depression.

The meanings assigned to colours also vary between professions. The table below gives two examples.

HOW DIFFERENT INDUSTRIES INTERPRET COLOURS		
	Financial services	Health Care
Blue	Reliable	Dead
Green	Money, profit	Infected, bilious
Yellow	Highlighted items important	Jaundiced
Red	Losses, unprofitable	Healthy
Source: adapted from Gerald E. Jones, *How To Lie with charts*, Sybex 1995.		

The logic of colour

Colour counts

A Xerox Corporation study showed that business documents in colour were read 70% quicker than documents in black and white. Also the study also found that recall error for the coloured documents was 39% lower than for black and white documents. The research found that most businesspeople interviewed agreed that the proper use of colour increased their speed, accuracy and comprehension of material.

Ronald E. Green in his article *The Persuasive Properties of Colour* argues that colour in presentations:

- Accelerates learning, retention and recall by between 55% and 78%.
- Improves and increases comprehension up to 73%.
- Increases recognition up to 78%.
- Increases motivation and participation up to 80%.
- Sells (products and ideas) more effectively by 50% to 85%.

Choosing colour combinations

To choose effective combinations we first need to understand the colour wheel. The wheel shows colours and their relationships. There are many possible colour wheels, but we will use a simple six colour version. The wheel has three primary colours (red, yellow and blue) and three secondary colours (orange, purple and green).

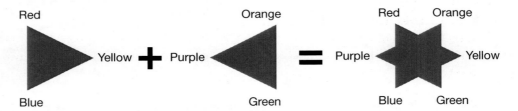

The most effective colour combinations are:

- Colours next to each other on the wheel.
- Colours opposite each other on the wheel.

It is important to understand that the impact of a colour is conditional. It can only be judged in the context of surrounding colours. We can obtain a more comprehensive understanding of colour combinations if we understand shades and tints. A shade is made by adding black to a pure colour. A tint is made by adding white to a pure colour.

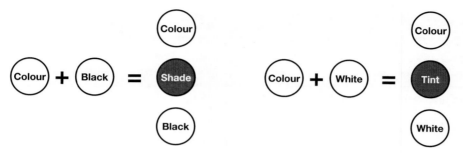

Some colours are better for shades and some colours are better for tints. Darker colours, such as red, purple and blue, suit shades; while lighter colours such as orange, yellow and green, are better for tints.

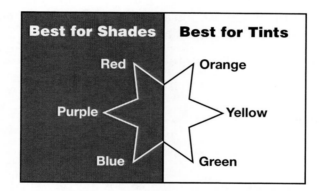

Now we understand about tints and shades, we can move from the colour wheel to look at the colour triangle. The colour triangle shows the relationship of pure colours, black and white and their intermediates (tints, shades and greys). Selecting colours along any axis of the triangle will produce good combinations. Very effective combinations for text and background are the twosomes shown with solid lines.

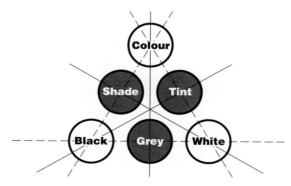

To sum up from the colour triangle, effective combinations of text and background are:

PREFERRED BASE COLOURS	A TWOSOME OF:	A TRIO OF:
Red, Purple or Blue	A shade with white,	A colour, shade and black.
Orange, Yellow or Green	A tint with black	A colour, tint and white.
Red, Purple, Blue, Orange, Yellow or Green	A pure colour with grey.	Black, white and grey.

If you want further information, Rob Carter's book *Working with Computer Type: Colour and Type* (1996) is a good source. Rob Carter devotes 50 colour pages to illustrating many of the combinations of text and background. Flicking through the pages shows the impact that different combinations create.

When combining colours, remember that 5% of the population are colour blind. Keep this in mind when using:

- Brown & Green,
- Blue & Purple
- Blue & Black.
- Red & Green.

Even though some of those colour combinations are very effective, you should be aware of the difficulties faced by a colour blind audience member, if you use those colours.

In summary, our suggestions are:

1. Use a twosome: shade with white; tint with black, pure colour with grey.
2. Alternatively, use a trio: colour, shade and black; colour, tint and white; black, white and grey.
3. Use colours next to each other on the wheel.
4. Use colours opposite each other on the wheel.

Finally, if you want a quick way to test colours, have a look at the colour match website (www.colormatch.dk). On this site you can make any colour from three primary colours and then see a palette of complimentary colours. We find this is a fast way to experiment with colours and find a palette to produce a theme for your presentation.

COLOUR TOOL: COLOSSAL SPORTS

Is there a colour commonly identified with the mood you wish to create?	No.
Is there a colour with a logical link to the content?	No.
Do you wish to link to company colours or company brand?	Use company colours, blue and white.
Identify the main colour for the background. Identify the colour of the text.	Blue background, white text.
Identify up to two other colours that will work well with your main colour.	Shades of blue, grey.
Three or less colours per slide?	Yes.
Do your colours look good once projected onto a screen?	Yes.

COLOUR TOOL: COMMUNITY GARDEN

Is there a colour commonly identified with the mood you wish to create?	Vibrant Green
Is there a colour with a logical link to the content?	Yes, Vibrant green—representing abundant nature
Do you wish to link to company colours or company brand?	No
Identify the main colour for the background. Identify the colour of the text.	Light shade of vibrant green for the main background with a strip of a picture of an abundant colourful garden on the left. Dark shade of green for the text
Identify up to two other colours that will work well with your main colour.	Vibrant Yellow and Red
Three or less colours per slide?	2–3
Do your colours look good once projected onto a screen?	yes

Insight 25
The Skilful Use of Images

"What doth it profit a man if he gains the whole world and loses his own soul?"

Jesus of Nazareth

Used skilfully, images can increase interest and participation, excite creativity, stir emotions and memories, provoke questions and uncover common ideas. In this insight and the next Insight, we will discuss the two approaches to using images in presentations: **the image as illustration** and **the interactive image**.

By understanding the subtle differences between the two approaches, when Persuading for Results you can select the most suitable approach, to maximise the persuasive effect. The method you choose will depend on the presentation style you choose, how much time you have to prepare and present, the size of your audience, the format of the presentation and how courageous you are.

Courage may seem like an unusual word to use. However, in persuasion people often prefer to use either logic or emotion. Those who prefer logic may not see an obvious reason why images are powerful persuaders. However, research shows that images trigger emotions and emotions trigger a different part of the brain to logical arguments. This maximises the impact of the persuasion.

When you understand the power of this concept, you will see that the most persuasive discussion in a one on one situation or a group meeting is when you combine logic and emotion. It touches everyone on the planet.

The image as illustration

Often an image is chosen by the presenter to illustrate and reinforce their words. This may be a photograph that shows a situation or a new product. Or the image might intensify the meaning of your words. For example, a photograph of a wrinkled, grey-haired man may appear on the screen as the presenter says, "As we grow old, our need for …"

With these examples, the audience is simply a passive viewer of the image. The presenter applies the meaning and the audience scrutinises the image for evidence of that meaning. The degree of persuasion depends on how clearly the image illustrates the point, so the Persuasive Presenter will ensure the image is almost a mirror of the verbal message.

To find good photographs, try typing "free stock photos" into your Google search. You can get ideas for photos by using Google Image search, simply type in a word and you will a diverse set of pictures. Remember to check whether the licensing allows you to use the photographs.

Professional sites where you can pay for photographs include:

www.istockphoto.com

www.shutterstock.com

www.gettyimages.com.au

While it is tempting to use Microsoft photographs, some of the images are becoming visual clichés: the handshake, passing the baton, group of business people, call centre operator, the globe, light bulb and chess pieces.

To persuade for results, take time to find fresh and interesting images to support your messages.

Insight 26
The Interactive Image

"You can learn a lot from people who view the world differently than you do."

Anthony J. D'Angelo

The Interactive Image

When using the image as an illustration, the presenter assigns a meaning to the image. In contrast, when using the 'interactive image' method the audience assigns a meaning to an image. There are three methods of the interactive approach:

1. Presenter's Image—Audience's Meaning.
2. Audience's Image—Audience's Meaning.
3. Common Image—Audience's Meaning.

The strength of these forms of the 'interactive image' is involving the audience because asking an audience to assign meaning to an image does four things:

- gets them involved in the content of your presentation.
- develops their understanding of your content.
- helps uncover issues.
- enables the presenter to understand and direct discussion.

For the interactive image approach to work, the presenter must assure participants that they will not be judged for their choice. This simply means saying, "Any image can mean anything to anyone. So just pick images that you believe represent the topic. We will not judge you for your choice—but we will be curious to hear the reasons behind it."

1. Presenter's Image-Audience's Meaning

In this first method of the interactive image, the presenter chooses the image and asks the audience to assign a meaning. This approach is useful for priming an audience to receive information, such as, the company's policies or a customer service model.

There are many possible interpretations of images, but there are usually several obvious ones. Consider the following example; You have been asked to present your company's 5-point customer service charter to a group of new employees.

You begin by holding up a poster-sized image of:	A young man in a supermarket uniform smiling as he kneels down to pick some loose groceries up off the floor of a shopping aisle. Beside him stands an older person watching him and smiling.
You deepen the interaction by asking the audience:	"What may have led the young man to help?" The group responds with: • A call over the speaker system from the floor manager. • The old man asked for help. • Another customer told him about it. • He may have immediately stopped what he was doing in the aisle and run over to help. • He may have anticipated the event from the other end of the aisle. • The old man waited, unnoticed for several minutes, until the young man, who is actually the store manager, came to his aid.
Now direct the conversation to the customer service charter:	"As you may know, our company has a 5-point customer service charter. At the top of this list is Exceed customer expectations. Thinking about this point, let's look at our hypothetical list and rank them in order from those most likely to exceed expectations to the least likely to exceed expectations."
You then proceed to anchor the best of these behaviours to this point of the charter and the image.	"It is obvious from our discussion that as that famous author and speaker Cathy De Vrye always says, 'Good service means good business.'"

While the charter is not changeable, the audience has an opportunity to get involved and to apply their ideals. This increases retention, and increases the probability the audience will recognise the real-life situation and act appropriately.

2. Audience's Image-Audience's Meaning

In this second method of the interactive image, the Persuasive Presenter allows the audience to select their own images for their own reasons. A simple way to do this is to hand each person a magazine or a wad of postcards and scissors, or CSS Cards© (as explained in detail later). Give them a topic, such as, "What do *you believe* are some of the characteristics of a good leader?" Ask them to go through the magazine and to find images that they believe represent the characteristics. Get them to cut the images out and place them on the table. When they finish, have them talk about their choices.

This method suits a workshop format because it will produce plenty of interaction between the presenter and the audience and among the audience. Like the first method of the interactive image, this second method is useful for preparing an audience to receive information.

When Persuading For Results, this method is particularly valuable when the presenter is raising issues and ideas that everybody is likely to have a strong opinion on, or when there is not necessarily a 'right' answer. It helps an audience to realise there are many different answers and gives them a richer understanding of the issue. Most importantly, it connects them directly to the issue with a meaning that is relevant to them.

The Persuasive Presenter recognises that most of what the audience needs to know, they already know—they just do not always recognise or apply this knowledge. This approach provides audience members with an opportunity to reflect on their own thoughts about a subject, and to compare these with the ideas of others.

It also primes people to *want* to hear what you have to say about the subject. After selecting images for their own reasons and articulating their choices, individuals want to assess their thinking against your expert opinion. You will need to be thoroughly prepared because each member of your audience is now looking for evidence that they have the 'most correct' understanding. In addition, audience members may be emotionally attached to their choices.

3. Common Image-Audience's Meaning

The third method of 'the interactive image' is the 'common image'. This special method has several features and benefits that warrant separate discussion.

The term 'common' describes two principal features:	All members of the audience are given a **common** (identical) set of images.
	The images are primarily **common** (of an everyday nature). They are like snapshots from a typical photo album, not the more directive marketing images found in magazines.
There are three persuasive benefits to using common images:	It encourages more heartfelt and natural responses from an audience. People are more comfortable giving a genuine, honest response when the image is common and not a strong marketing image.
	People find personal and emotional meanings in the images. This increases their commitment to their responses and improves the quality of their participation. Again, a better connection between the audience and the subject improves the presenter's opportunity for persuasion.
	The images are suitable for many presentations, including business and nonbusiness presentations.

A simple way to use this third interactive method is to hand each person a deck of cards, with each card containing an image. Give them a topic, such as, "What do *you believe* are some of the characteristics of a good leader?" Ask them to look through the deck of images to find the four pictures they believe represent the characteristics. Get them to place them on the table after several minutes. When they finish, have them talk about their choices.

Using common images in this way is fun and:

- reduces tension and encourages full participation. All members recognise that they have the same tool for expression as their colleagues and feel on par with other members, regardless of the levels of experience or rank.
- encourages and simplifies comparisons between group members.
- quickly highlights common choices and unique choices across a group.
- helps the group agree quickly.
- enables discussion about priorities and preferences by individuals placing their choices in order of preference before comparing them with others.
- promotes interest and respect for other people's perspectives.
- It is fun.

To use the 'common image concept', a presenter could prepare their own set of images using reproductions of photographs and graphics. However, it is more practical and efficient to use a commercially available system—**The Compatibility Communication System (or CCS)**. The CCS developers coined the term 'common image communication concept' and their system provides everything the Persuasive Presenter needs to benefit from this approach in their presentations. You can find out more from their website: www.ccscorporation.com.au, and from the case study below.

Case Study: State Street in Japan

When Vicky Karatasas, who is now the Head of HR for the Commonwealth Bank, was at State Street as Vice President, Head of Leadership and Change—Europe, she was responsible for employees' career opportunities at a Regional level. This role brought many challenges as she managed staff development in a range of business and cultural contexts.

The following story is about Vicky's experiences presenting to a group of business people in Japan. The story illustrates the power of images to provoke thought, to break down barriers between people, and to promote communication.

Vicky travelled to Japan to run workshops with Japanese State Street employees. She had researched the local business culture in Japan and understood the Japanese are well-known for their work ethic and strong group relationships. She had also been advised that the Japanese participants were likely to be reluctant about voicing their difficulties and frustrations in front of their colleagues. She understood the participants were also unlikely to speak openly about their own underperformance or that of their colleagues. She was concerned because she knew that without frank and open communication, it would be difficult to solve the challenges facing the Japanese teams. Fortunately, Vicky used a creative technique the CCS cards©, involving images, to provoke constructive, open discussion. She tells her story in the following.

A Picture Paints a Thousand Words

The workshops and presentations that I gave in Japan were very important, from a business perspective. So, I developed a backup plan before I went to Japan, in case my initial queries about personal and group performance did not work. In the first workshop, when my questions were met with awkward silence, I realised I had been right to prepare a more creative ice-breaker.

I introduced my creative ice-breaker by distributing CCS cards to all the participants. I asked everyone to go through their pack and select a card that depicted something unique about themselves. After several minutes, I asked each participant to put their cards on the table and stand up and walk around the room, viewing everyone else's cards. I then asked each person to pick a card that had been selected by one of their peers and share with the group what they interpreted it to mean.

One employee had selected a card with an image of an empty baseball diamond. His peer, who was asked to share his interpretation of the card, said the card probably represented the person's love of baseball. As it turned out, the card represented something completely different. The employee who had selected the card explained the image represented his inability to get his colleagues to work together, like a team. Sometimes it felt like they were not even on the same field! As the employee talked about this, he referred to the image, extending the metaphor to include reference to himself as the coach and his boss as the referee. Other employees commented that customers are actually referees, because the customer has the final say on the success of the team. This provoked discussion about the different pressures and systems of accountability faced by the employees.

As I watched, I realised the metaphor inspired by the image allowed the employee to talk about his work indirectly. It also captured the attention of his colleagues and prompted them to draw comparisons with their own experience.

When I asked this individual to then share with the group what his biggest challenge was with his team, he quickly reached for a different card. It was an image of a marching band. He laughed and said he wanted to have all his team members marching to the same tune. Another colleague laughed and said, "I don't! I am tone deaf, so it would be a disaster." Everyone laughed. One by one, the participants shared their interpretations of the various images in a nonthreatening, constructive atmosphere.

Since then, I have used the cards many times with people from diverse cultural backgrounds. I think the creative use of images can break down barriers more effectively than most other methods.

Vicky comments the cards have worked for her in different cultural contexts. Imagine that you were asked to present to a group of doctors in Poland, or to a group of exchange students from China. What would an audience of Polish doctors expect? What would Chinese students expect? How would you begin preparing for this? Let's look at the lessons we can take from Vicky's story and adapt to your own presentations.

Lesson 1: Have a good understanding of your audience's culture. Researching Japanese culture allowed Vicky to tailor her presentation. See *Insight 8—Understand your Audience and Insight 12—Consider Culture.*

Lesson 2: Involve your audience. Vicky created a friendly environment where her audience members could share and learn in a non confrontational environment. See *Insight 27—Involve Your Audience.*

Lesson 3: Use different activities to enhance your presentation. The use of image cards stimulated the audience members to think and communicate. See *Insight 27—Involve Your Audience.*

Insight 27
Involve Your Audience

"Learning is not a spectator sport."
Malcolm Knowles

When Persuading For Results, involving your audience throughout your presentation helps maintain their attention. Indeed, self-discovery and practical application is often the most effective way of learning and the most effective way of persuading. There are many ways to involve people, depending on the size of your audience. You may like to give people an opportunity to test your product, or to have them work with your ideas actively. Make sure the activity you use is linked back to your message. The activity should reinforce your message, not distract from it.

Use Imagery

An activity that we like to use in our presentations is showing a visual image and asking the audience what they see. We allow a minute for people to write down their responses. Then we ask five or six people for their answers, or we have people discuss with others what they wrote. Everyone's interpretation will be slightly different. People are usually surprised at the different responses. To them it is obvious what the picture is of, and they had not considered alternative interpretations. This shows our audience that to understand clients you need to consider their perspective, which may be different from your perspective. Rather than simply describing this, people have a chance to experience it for themselves.

Ask Thought Provoking Questions

A second method for involving your audience is to probe them with questions. Instead of quoting a fact or statistic, sometimes it can be more effective to pose it as a question. For example in a presentation on food preservation, you might ask "What is the only food that does not go off?" This will start the audience thinking, increasing their awareness of the issue, as they logically try to find the answer. Their intrigue will mount as they try to find the answer. Their motivation will increase too. Then, ask for a few answers before revealing the correct answer — honey. The audience will be primed to hear all about the amazing composition of honey. This is much more effective than simply saying, "Honey is the only food that does not go off".

Statistics by themselves can be quite dry and uninteresting. Turning them into questions involves the audience. However, when you activate your audience members' minds, you risk having your ideas challenged. So, be prepared to provide the evidence behind your statement. If someone challenges you, do not shy away because it shows that they are listening to you. You have made them think, and they are simply voicing their concerns. This is the perfect opportunity for you to clear up any misunderstandings.

Use Quotation as a Springboard

Like questions, quotations can provide a good source of discussion. Present a quotation that is linked directly to your message and ask the audience for their interpretations of it. The quotation should be directly related to your topic, once again guiding the audience to the point of your topic.

Use these techniques by either asking a few members of the audience for their answers, or by dividing the audience into groups where they share their answers with others. Using groups is ideal for building group relationships within your audience, doubling as a 'get to know you' activity.

Visualise

Helping the audience visualise a situation can be an effective way of involving the audience without relying on expensive resources or time-consuming preparation. A colleague of ours recently gave a presentation on optimism to a group of fifty schoolteachers. The presenter was one of about ten people presenting that day. Her presentation was late in the afternoon. She suspected that by this time their attention span would be short, so she decided to begin by stimulating their imaginations.

Before the audience knew what the topic was, she asked them all to imagine a scenario where a student was misbehaving. The presenter went into some detail about the situation and then asked the teachers to imagine their reaction. They were all asked to write down exactly what they would say to the child. She then told them to put what they had written aside until later.

The presenter went on to introduce the topic and talked about using positive communication. She talked about the psychological patterns of children and the effect of an 'optimistic style' of discipline. Her message was logical and powerful. Then she asked people to look over what they had written at the beginning of the session and to critique their own response, noting where they had displayed symptoms of pessimism.

Once people were aware of negativity, they could identify it in their own behaviour. Many teachers were amazed at their pessimistic approach to discipline. Had they not done this exercise before, the teachers probably would have thought, "I don't do that. This is not relevant to my behaviour." The exercise allowed the audience to be more self-aware and provided an opportunity for them to apply their learning immediately.

Give Surprise Gifts

A fun method that we sometimes see used in presentations is taping an item to the bottom of the seats in the audience. This is particularly good for longer presentations, spicing up the session by asking midway that everyone look under their seats. Depending on how much money you want to spend, the object can be anything from a lolly to a copy of your latest book.

Readers familiar with *The Oprah Show* will be aware of Oprah Winfrey's use of this technique. Midway through a session with a guest speaker Oprah will ask her audience members to look under their chairs. The mood in the studio becomes electric as people scream with glee at discovering a free beauty product or self-help book.

Use Your Creativity — find an activity

Incorporating an activity into your presentation is a powerful way of building rapport with the audience. It will keep the audience stimulated and will drive home your message. There are many ways to do this, so you will have to use your creativity to come up with an activity that suits your presentation. A good source of activities is the series of books by Scannell and Newstrom, *Games Trainers Play*.

INVOLVE THE AUDIENCE TOOL	
How can I use imagery?	
What questions can I ask?	
How can I use quotations?	
How can I help the audience visualise?	
How can I use surprise gifts?	
How can I build activity into the presentation?	

Insight 28
Your Image

"If wrinkles must be written upon our brows, let them not be written upon the heart. The spirit should not grow old."

James A. Garfield

First Impressions

When persuading, before you have even opened your mouth the audience will begin to make judgements about you. Their first impressions of you will be based on your image.

Personal appearance is a sensitive issue for most people. You might say, "If the content of my presentation is good and my style is professional and effective, my personal appearance should not matter." True, you should not try to win over your audience with your appearance—you are a trying to give a professional presentation, not a glitzy performance.

So, instead of thinking about personal appearance as impressing the audience, think of it as an important key to not distracting them. Think about whether having four rings on each finger will distract the audience, or whether a multicoloured fluorescent tie will divert attention from your message.

What to wear

There are various opinions on how presenters should dress. The truth is, as fashion changes, so do the rules about appropriate clothes for presenters. For example, big shoulder pads were standard 'power-wear' for women in the 1980s. By the 1990s, shoulder pads were less common. Scarves come in and out of fashion, as do pinstripe suits.

The one rule that does not change is that a presenter should always be neat and well groomed. For women this means neat and manicured nails, polished shoes, tidy hair and stockings without ladders. Men should make sure they have clean nails, polished shoes, straight ties and wrinkle free shirts. Both men and women should be careful that their clothes are not too small, or too big.

As a rule, err on the side of discretion and modesty. Loud flashy colours and revealing clothing will detract from the credibility of both male and female presenters.

To ensure that your wardrobe is not giving you a stale image, ask a trustworthy friend to comment on your wardrobe. However, do not get angry if they suggest that you need a change.

A good way to determine how to dress appropriately is to take note of what the people who are senior to you at work wear. If you want to move up the corporate ladder, dress like you belong on the next tier. You do not necessarily have to spend a lot of money. You can buy good quality clothes on sale, or you can buy quality items, but less of them.

Dress for Success

Simple rules include:	Have regular haircuts.
	Wear classic, tailored lines.
	Dress modestly.
	Keep clothes crumple free (hang your jacket up in the car to avoid crushing).
	Keep your shoes shiny and your belt in good shape.
	Check for perspiration stains under your arms.
	Wear only a small amount of jewellery.
	Have your clothes tailored for a perfect fit.
Our advice for men:	Keep your jacket buttoned when standing or walking.
	Wear matching belt and shoes.
	Do not wear loud ties or ties with cartoon characters.
	Wear conservative socks that will not expose skin when you cross your legs.
Our advice from a female colleague for women:	Wear shoes that cover the toe and are comfortable to walk in.
	If you wear makeup, keep it subtle and neutral.
	Carry a spare pair of stockings.
	If you wear knee-high stockings under trousers, make sure they don't slide down around your ankles.

One final word of advice about clothing is to consider keeping a spare change of clothes in your office, or carrying a spare set with you. Just days before this book was completed, we saw a presenter spill a super-sized mug of coffee straight down her white blouse, moments before taking the stage. Without a spare change of clothes, she had little choice but to take the stage in a woolly winter coat. The audience members, all of whom were wearing short sleeves, could not understand why she was dressed for sub-zero temperatures.

More than clothes

Apart from clothes, other aspects of your physical appearance send signals to your audience. If you are tired and red-eyed, your audience will have the same response to your message.

Body language also plays a large role in your image. Your stance, for example, will tell the audience a lot about you. Your stance can be influenced by the physical environment, such as a lectern, but don't let this be an excuse for poor posture. Generally, it is best to stand straight, make open gestures with your arms and hands, and look happy and interested in both your message and your audience. See *Insight 29—Body Language*, for more tips on the use of body language.

Insight 29
Body Language

"We judge our intentions, but others judge our actions."

William Moulton Marston

Research suggests that body language accounts for two thirds of communication. Therefore, body language can make or break a presentation. To some degree, your body language is set in place, but there are several simple tips to help you.

Eye contact

When you are making contact with people, it is natural to look at them almost constantly. Most people do this during normal conversation.

Generally, most of us find it easier to talk to others one-on-one rather than to a group of people. That is because you can use the normal rhythms of speech, and use your body language to relate to people. When Persuading For Results, your job is to try to transfer the intimacy of that one-on-one situation to an audience.

Rather than sweeping your gaze over the audience constantly, it is more effective to pick out one person at a time. Make your selection from different sections of the audience and look directly at the chosen person, for a full sentence or two. You will build a rapport with that person, and appear more genuine to the audience as a whole. Vary your eye contact between four or five spots around the room. These people will become proxies for the entire audience.

Making eye contact can be intimidating. To make it easier, greet people as they enter the room. Linger to talk with a few friendly people. Then, when you begin your presentation, seek out these friendly, familiar faces. Start by making eye contact with these people and as your confidence grows you can broaden your gaze to take in the rest of the audience.

Facial expressions

Herbert Samuels put it the best when he said, "The world is like a mirror; frown at it and it frowns at you. Smile and it smiles too." Your face is a powerful tool for communication. Even if you have perfected your speech, appearance and gestures, you will not win the audience over without a smile. A smile is easy to do, and the dividends far outweigh the effort.

Start your presentation with a wide, friendly and sincere smile. It will be infectious. Your smile will put the audience in a positive frame of mind, and may even fool you into a state of relaxed confidence; the more you smile, the better the rapport between you and your audience. However, your smile must be sincere. Practice smiling in front of the mirror. Get to know how a sincere smile makes your face feel so that you can recognise a false smile without a mirror.

Psychologists have shown that smiling releases serotonin into your brain. Serotonin is the chemical in the brain that gives us a natural feeling of pleasure, peace and well-being. So, a genuine smile will in fact make you feel more relaxed and positive.

A smile is not the only powerful facial expression. An arched eyebrow can signal scepticism, wide eyes can indicate surprise and a furrowed brow can show deep contemplation. Practice using different facial expressions—this is a chance to let your dramatic instincts take over and to captivate the audience's attention.

Gestures

The most effective presenter uses his or her entire body to communicate. The first step is to have a good posture. Stand up straight and balance your weight on both feet. Theoretically, the field for your gestures is as far as your arms will stretch, as high as your arms will reach and as long as your legs will stride. In a small room with a small audience, you may want to make your gestures subtle, but in a large room with a large audience, you can use more dramatic gestures.

Many presenters use the same tired gestures. Through overuse, the technique of upturned palms to show honesty has become redundant, so avoid 'textbook' gestures. Be creative and look for dramatic images that can be expressed through body language. You may find it helpful to watch someone communicate in sign language. This provides great ideas on how to communicate with gestures. It may also be helpful to videotape your presentations to see how you can improve.

Just as gestures can add to your presentation, fidgeting or awkward movement can detract from it. If your hands are shaking from nervousness, resist the urge to clench your fists. This will make you seem anxious or even aggressive. Do not keep your hands in your pockets, or wring them. Do not fidget with rings, watches, pens or your hair. If you are uncertain about what to do with your hands, and there is a podium, just rest them lightly on the podium. Watching yourself in the mirror or on video will help you to pick up any unconscious mannerisms that you use.

Getting better

Sometimes we are not aware that we have gestures or facial expressions that may irritate, annoy or distract. If you can, video tape a presentation or a practice and then review the tape. Alternatively, ask a friend, "Do I use any gestures or facial expressions that might irritate, annoy or distract an audience?" Write down whatever they say and do not argue with them. At first, do not try to change, but simply count how many times you use this gesture in a presentation or ask a friend to do this for you. Often just being more aware by counting the gesture will help eliminate it quickly.

Insight 30
Voice

"Whatever you can do or dream, you can begin it. Boldness has genius, power, and magic in it."

Goethe

Do you remember the first time you heard yourself on tape? Did you think, "That is not how I sound. It must be a bad recording!" Perhaps you were shocked to discover your nasal twang, your monotonous tone or your singsong speech patterns.

Very few people are truly aware of the weaknesses of their own vocal and speech patterns. However, as a presenter, you must come to terms with the problems and the potential of your vocal style.

The first step is to listen to yourself on tape, no matter how painful and embarrassing this is. Record yourself reading out a newspaper article or talking to one of your friends. Compare your own voice to the voices of your friends, actors and television journalists. You should discover that low voices are easier to listen to than high-pitched voices.

The first step to making effective use of your voice comes with the decision about whether or not to use a microphone. If you have to raise your voice at all to be heard, consider using a microphone. This will prevent your voice sounding forced and aggressive, and will minimise long-term damage to your vocal chords.

Pitch

Among the most irritating problems is a high-pitched voice. This is particularly common among women, but can also be a problem for men. Also a constantly high-pitched voice, inflecting upwards at the end of a sentence can undermine the presenter's authority by suggesting the statement is a question. It can make the most competent and confident presenter appear to be seeking the audience's approval.

You can learn to control the pitch of your voice through practice. Practice humming in a low tone in the shower, or singing a low harmony with your favourite song while driving the car. Practice reciting your favourite dramatic poem in a low, whispered voice, or read the part of your favourite male Shakespearean character.

You can also improve your control over your voice by strengthening your diaphragm. To do this, lie on your back and place telephone books (or even just your hands) on your diaphragm. Breathe in and out slowly to strengthen your diaphragm. Actors and actresses use similar activities to strengthen their voices. Another activity you can do to warm up your voice is by repeating the word "gudabuda" as fast and as many times as you can. Follow this with "budaguda". This difficult to pronounce sound will exercise your tongue, lips and vocal chords.

Enunciation

There are few things as frustrating as listening to a speaker mumble and slur their way through an important presentation. The audience has to listen a lot harder to understand a presenter who fails to articulate clearly. The result will be a tired and irritated audience. Listen to yourself on tape and ask your family and friends to tell you when you are mumbling. Be particularly wary when you are tired or rushed, because that is when you are most likely to mumble.

Breathing

An important aspect of vocal control is breathing correctly. Breathing slowly and deeply into the lungs increases the flow of oxygen into your body, which has a twofold effect. First, the flow of blood to the brain is increased, helping you think more clearly. Second, the flow of air into the vocal chords will improve, resulting in clearer speech.

Getting Better

In summary, we suggest four ways to improve: record your voice, ask a friend for feedback, get a drama/voice coach or find the tape series *The Sound of Your Voice* by Dr Carol Fleming.

Insight 31
Your Language

"Dare to be different."
Phil Crothers

The words you use tell the audience a great deal about you. Is your language colloquial? Is it highly technical? Do you use long, complicated sentences, or short, sharp sentences? Do you use unnecessarily long words?

To a certain extent, your language habits are firmly in place. You might use colloquial phrases without even noticing. For example, you might not even notice that you say 'yeah' instead of 'yes'. The audience might not be so quick to overlook it. The good news is it is never too late to improve your language habits. You can avoid falling into several easily identified traps.

Colloquial language

The first step is related to people who are new speakers of a language. New language speakers often remark that colloquial expressions are the hardest aspect of a language to master. If you use expressions that are unfamiliar to some audience members, you will isolate and frustrate them. If you do catch yourself using such phrases, quickly stop and rephrase. Think about the pace of your delivery. Slow down your speech, and simplify your words.

Jargon

Most professions have their own language, comprised of technical jargon. For example, computer programmers talk about XML, and Linux. It can be difficult for a layperson to communicate within this subculture if they are not fluent in the language. While jargon can make communication more efficient for members within a subculture, it can exclude nonmembers from participating effectively.

If you really must use technical jargon, at least give your audience a 'cushion'. The first time you use the term, explain it thoroughly. If you can, relate it to a simpler, better-known term. If you mention it again, use it in a context that makes it as clear as possible. Do this with all the jargon you use. For example, do not assume that because you have being saying 'ASEAN' for years that your audience will know you are talking about the Association of South East Asian Nations.

Offensive Language

Another easy mistake to avoid is the use of potentially offensive language. Some forms of language are obviously inappropriate. For example, swearing during a presentation will almost never be appropriate, even if you swear amongst your colleagues.

Offensive language can often be more subtle than simply swearing. Read the following statements and see if you can pick what might be potentially offensive.

Teacher: "When I am speaking to the parent of one of my students, I like to ask what expectations she has for her child's progress."

CEO: "I am looking for a new manager who will speak his mind."

The first statement suggests that only mothers are actively involved in educating their children. This is potentially offensive to both men and women. The second statement assumes the new manager must be male. Simple and unremarkable statements like these can spell disaster. Avoid terms that imply that certain occupations and roles are gender specific. Instead of chairman, say chairperson, instead of stewardess use flight attendant.

Gender is not the only potential minefield. You should also be aware of the way you talk about age, ethnicity, marital status, religion, disability, culture and sexuality. Reflection and restraint using language can prevent disasters.

Pauses

Pauses can be incredibly effective. When you pause, people look at you immediately. They hear the break in transmission and wonder what is coming next. Pauses assist with transition, or can be used for dramatic effect.

Train yourself to pause rather than saying 'um' or 'ah'. Even if you forget where you are up to, a pause while you stop to recollect is better than an embarrassed "Uh—I just have to look at my notes to see where I am up to." A five second pause is plenty of time for you to remember, and at the end of that time you will have everyone's attention focused firmly on you.

Words are tools

Choose your tools carefully. Use vivid language that will stir the emotions. Strunk and White's advice for writers sums it up well:

"Write with nouns and verbs, not with adjectives and adverbs. The adjective hasn't been built that can pull a weak or inaccurate noun out of a tight place."

Use active language, use verbs, and talk about real things not abstractions. If you want action at the end of the presentation use an active style. For example do not say "After your completion of the registration process, implementation of the guidelines should be accomplished immediately" say "after registering, implement the guidelines."

Helpful Hints

- Avoid sloppy grammar. Instead of, "I am real pleased", say, "I am very pleased." *The Economist Style Guide* at www.economist.com gives some useful tips.
- Use positive language. Research in psychology shows that people understand and recall positively worded sentences more quickly and accurately than negatively worded ones. For example, people will respond better to "Treat people with respect" than "Do not treat people with disrespect".
- Repeat key words.
- Check your presentation for statements or words that may offend or intimidate your audience.
- Erase "um", "ah" and "err" from your vocabulary.

Getting Better

Use similar techniques to those suggested for body language. Record yourself on tape or ask a friend to tell you if use phrases that might irritate, annoy or distract an audience. Then monitor how many times you use that phrase in a presentation or ask a friend to do this for you. Often just being more aware of the phrase by counting how many times you use the phrase will quickly eliminate the problem. We recall one colleague who reduced his use of the word 'basically' from 40 times per hour to four times per hour by asking a friendly member of the audience to record how many times he used the word. This raised his awareness so much that the problem quickly disappeared.

Insight 32
Questions, Suggestions and Options

"The important thing is not to stop questioning."

Albert Einstein

Questions

Some of the best persuaders—salesmen, negotiators and psychiatrists—persuade with questions rather than statements. Questions raise awareness and direct the attention of the audience. If we ask you to rate the tension in your shoulders on a scale of 1–10 with 1 as low and 10 as the highest, it is impossible for you to avoid becoming aware of the tension in your shoulders. The power of questions to generate action and commitment is displayed well in John Whitmore's book *Coaching for Performance*. We suggest that you should collect good questions.

One question to avoid is Why? It produces a defensive response because it is a blame question. Few people will answer this question truthfully and often it will damage the rapport of a presentation or conversation. Other ways to ask the same question are, "What were your reasons for that?" or "How did you decide to do that?"

Neil Rackham, a psychologist, found that skilled negotiators used questions twice as often as average negotiators. Rackham went on to research successful sales people and developed a sales method based on studying 35,000 sales calls. The essence of the method is four different kinds of questions: situation, problem, implication and need-benefit. Questions are useful for other forms of persuasion as well as sales. What questions can you use to persuade?

Suggestions

What is the difference between presenting information as a statement, and making a suggestion? Peter Honey a psychologist and expert on behaviour, suggests a listener has four possible reactions to a statement:

1. To support the statement.
2. To build on the idea.
3. To seek more information.
4. To state a difficulty.

His research on behaviour indicates using suggestions will increase the chances of a proposal being accepted and reduce the chances of the listener finding a difficulty with it.

Clearly, listeners will not accept a proposal that does not meet their needs. However, if the language we use influences human behaviour then when Persuading For Results, you can use the tool of language to increase the chances of action. Peter Honey found using suggestions doubles the chance the listener will support your proposal and reduces by four the chance of a difficulty. Using suggestions will not stop a listener rejecting a bad proposal, but it will increase the chances of a listener accepting a good proposal.

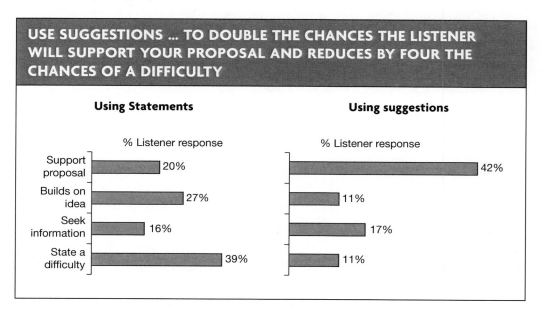

USE SUGGESTIONS ... TO DOUBLE THE CHANCES THE LISTENER WILL SUPPORT YOUR PROPOSAL AND REDUCES BY FOUR THE CHANCES OF A DIFFICULTY

Using Statements

% Listener response

Support proposal	20%
Builds on idea	27%
Seek information	16%
State a difficulty	39%

Using suggestions

% Listener response

Support proposal	42%
Builds on idea	11%
Seek information	17%
State a difficulty	11%

Negotiation expert Roger Fisher recognises the power of questions and suggestions to influence others and makes three suggestions:

1. Ask others to contribute their opinions.
2. Offer your thoughts, but present them as suggestions, or one way of acting, not 'the' way.
3. Do something constructive.

Fisher's second point leads us to our final suggestion to present options then a recommendation, rather than simply a recommendation.

Options

Robert Miller and Stephen Heiman discuss the psychology of selling in their book *Conceptual Selling*. They indicate that people follow a consistent process to make decisions:

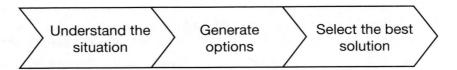

Understand the situation → Generate options → Select the best solution

If this is how people think, then using this process makes it easier for them. Missing out the second step may seem to save time, but you run the risk of the audience generating options and selecting a different solution to the one you recommend. Far better to follow the process, present options and then guide the audience to the reasons for the solution that you recommend.

Insight 33
Use Handouts

*"Have more than thou showest,
speak less than thou knowest."*

Shakespeare

A handout is a summary of your presentation the audience walks away with. It helps frame the audience's memories of the presentation. When Persuading For Results, handouts can enhance your professional image. They can also help your audience spend more time listening and less time writing.

Imagine you have been asked to persuade the executive committee to allocate surplus funds to your business unit. Your research reveals four other managers will be presenting to the same group. You also glean the other presenters will just attend the meeting and talk to the group. This is a great opportunity to prepare a visual presentation and make a superior impact.

Prepare your presentation and handout at the same time and you will save time and create a closely integrated package. A good way to plan is to draw a line down the centre of your page and plan your presentation and handouts simultaneously.

Handouts are a good place to put:	Charts and diagrams—statistical data that is too detailed for your visuals.
	Case studies—to show a working example of your message.
	Web sites—relevant references for audience members to find more information.
	Samples—to let your audience test your product or service.
	Magazine, journal and newspaper articles.
	Presentation slides—to enable people to scribble around your notes.

When Persuading For Results, everything in the handout should influence the audience to take the action you recommend.

Your handouts reflect your presentation, and it also reflects on you. An audience, persuaded by your polished and dynamic presentation, might walk away with a different impression if your handouts are unhelpful, boring, inaccurate or disorganised. They might also pass the handout on to colleagues, multiplying the detrimental impact of the handouts.

The key to deciding what to include in your handouts is to think about the specific message you want the audience to take away. Do not bombard them with facts and figures that do not relate directly to your ultimate goal: the action you recommend.

Here are some handy hints:

Distribution

- Give the audience time to leaf through your handouts before you start.
- If you are running a group workshop, consider whether to make your handouts interactive so the audience has to fill in missing words as they listen.
- Make sure you have enough copies.
- If the handouts are supporting information, tell the audience you will hand them out at the end. Do not give them something to read that distracts them from what you have to say or pre-empts your presentation.
- If handouts are to be distributed during your presentation, organise helpers to do this quickly.
- Do not let handouts be a distraction before you finish.

Format

- Sift through all your information and only include what is relevant. If you end up with a lot of material, sort it so people can see what is directly related to the topic and what is additional information.
- Be concise—as a general rule, handouts should be no more than ten pages long.
- Use good quality paper and printing. Paper heavier than the standard $80g/m^2$ creates a subtle impression of quality. Try $100g/m^2$ and feel the difference.
- Number or colour-code the pages so that you can direct the audience to the relevant page quickly.
- Make your handouts attractive and easy to read—a clear typestyle, distinct divisions between content and headings, plenty of space, and a graphic or two for clarity and interest.
- Ensure sufficient space to write. Narrow margins will frustrate enthusiastic audience members, and give lazy people permission to be passive.
- Provide folders with your company name and their company name for the audience to store their notes in. Months later, you want them to be able to remember your name.

HANDOUTS TOOL: COLOSSAL SPORTS	
Are they a summary or supplementary?	Supplementary.
Are they interactive working notes?	No.
Timing of distribution	Will provide them at the conclusion of presentation.
Include statistics or just insights?	Both.
Include articles or case studies?	Yes, include the case study from Bloom Consulting.
Magazine articles?	Will include the article, "Good Systems are Good Business" from The Herald, March 2010, page 4.
Will you include your presentation slides?	No.
Will you allow flicking time at start?	No.
Will you allow room to write?	Yes, to encourage them to use as reference material later in other meetings.

Will you include graphics?	Will include graphs used in my presentation, and any illustrations.
Will you use helpers to distribute?	No.
How many pages will you include?	Ten.

HANDOUTS TOOL: COMMUNITY GARDEN

Are they a summary or supplementary?	Summary
Are they interactive working notes?	No
Timing of distribution	After introduction
Include statistics or just insights?	Some Statistics
Include articles or case studies?	Newspaper articles of other community gardens in nearby areas
Magazine articles?	Add as an appendix the article on the benefits of a community garden from Community Harvest magazine volume 3
Will you include your presentation slides?	No
Will you allow flicking time at start?	No
Will you allow room to write?	Yes
Will you include graphics?	Some—print on coloured paper for greater effect
Will you use helpers to distribute?	No
How many pages will you include?	Less than 10

Insight 34
Tell Stories

*"In marketing, a good product is important —
the right price will help —
but there's no substitute for a great story."*

David Nomchong

A story or a metaphor is a persuasive use of words because stories persuade with emotion. Until recently, business communicators often neglected stories. However, if you look in your local bookshop now you will see a growing number of business books that include stories. Ken Blanchard pioneered a series of books teaching management in a story form, starting with the *One Minute Manager*. Also, Annette Simmons wrote *The Story Factor—Inspiration, influence and persuasion through the art of storytelling*. In support of storytelling she asserts that:

> **"In order to learn about influence we must leave the comfort of models, sequences, and step-by-step recipes. The magic of influence is more in what we say and who we are. This 'how/who' stuff defies categories, definition and rational analysis. Influence results from how others feel about you and your goals. In the realm of feeling and emotions (by definition: irrational), ideas aren't organised in a traditional sense."**

To persuade for results, we urge you to use stories. Some persuaders will be uncomfortable with this, but we suggest you start by watching and listening to people who are good persuaders and notice how often they use stories. Some of the best persuaders, salesmen, negotiators and psychiatrists, counsellors and consultants persuade with stories and metaphors.

A careful choice of metaphor can be very persuasive. For the business world, Sue Knight, discusses metaphors in her practical book, *NLP at Work*:

> "Excellent communicators and influencers use metaphor to capture and hold attention... Metaphors have been with us in many forms for as long as we can remember. Stories in the form of fairy tales, proverbs, and parables are passed down from generation to generation. Metaphors are so rooted in our upbringing that for many people they act as an anchor for relaxation and involvement. So, metaphors bypass any conscious blocks or resistance and slip into the unconscious mind. The unconscious mind responds to the challenge of the metaphor by finding a unique solution that fits the listener's experience and needs."

Imagine that you work for a company that has a problem competing in the marketplace because they are focused internally and rarely consider the needs of the customer or the actions of competitors. How would you persuade them to change their perspective?

Companies like this often view the company as a big machine—turn this handle or press this button and the results they want will come out. Combined with the obvious methods of data and logic, the metaphor can be used to persuade. Here the Persuasive Presenter might suggest that the senior managers currently think of the company as a machine and discuss some of the implications of this. Then the presenter might go on to suggest another way to look at the company is as an ocean-going racing yacht. Here the winds are the needs of the customer that change and alter with time. The tides are the actions of the competitors that also change. If the financial target of the business is the destination, how do we steer the company there? The captain of the yacht will monitor the winds and tides regularly and the crew adjust the sails to ensure they reach the destination. The presenter might ask what this means for the company, what changes do we need to make to ensure our yacht gets to its destination?

Changing the metaphor that people use is a powerful way to influence individuals and organisations. For presenters who wish to change organisations, Gareth Morgan's books, such as *Images of Organisations*, are challenging reading and offer different metaphors.

Choosing Good Stories

Choosing good stories has become much easier ever since the publication of *Made To Stick* by Heath and Heath, 2007. This book analyses what makes stories memorable and finishes with a checklist of what makes stories sticky and memorable. The checklist is a useful way to choose stories to support your message.

Another useful tool is the story matrix introduced by Craig Wortmann in his book *What's your Story?: Using stories to ignite performance and be more successful (2006)*. The story matrix is a table to collect stories to persuade for a particular purpose. Down the side of the table are four story types—success, failure, fun and legends. Success stories show what's important to be successful; failure stories help others learn how to improve their performance too. Fun stories, are real-life events when things go wrong or unexpected things happen, making us smile or laugh. Legends are stories from outside or inside the business you have heard many times, stories that inspire or remind about something important.

Across the top of the table are the five areas that you are trying to influence. The book uses the example of five leadership skills: culture, execution, sales, service, teamwork and managing yourself. So, with five leadership skills and four different kind of story, there are spaces for 20 possible stories about leadership. In each of the 20 spaces, you can write a brief version of the story, then the lessons from the story and then applications for the story.

Not every space in the story matrix needs to be filled. As long as there is a least one story in each column, then you can use stories to persuade. Once you have created the story matrix, then in this example when you want to persuade somebody about leadership, then you would scan the story matrix and pick a story or two before you met them.

The story matrix adds some structure to using stories and ensures you capture the best stories and use the best stories to be a more persuasive presenter.

Insight 35
Delivering Bad News

"Even when confronted with a hopeless situation, you still have a chance to make life meaningful ... in turning personal tragedy into a triumph or by transforming your predicament to an accomplishment."

Victor Frankl

Not all presentations are about promoting great ideas or fabulous products. Sometimes you may not be particularly excited about sharing your news with your audience. There may be times when you are responsible for delivering bad news to a group. Imagine being asked to announce to a company that half of the staff will be retrenched. With accelerating change around the world we see presenters delivering bad news more often. Mergers and acquisitions, rationalisation and redundancies mean presenters must be skilful in delivering bad news.

David Nomchong, international motivational speaker and the author of the bestselling book on bad news, "Leukaemia: a minor inconvenience," shares his thoughts on how to deal with bad news. The book allows you to feel how the audience would feel with bad news and then what needs to be done to shift their thinking on what to do next.

Don't Shoot the Messenger

In these situations, the natural reaction of the audience is often to hold the presenter responsible for the news. Therefore, it is important to present the message independently from yourself. You should not point the blame at someone else. But you should try to detach yourself from the message and empathise with the audience—put yourself on their side by saying something like, "I know this is terrible news. I am unhappy about this too". This way it will be the message versus you and your audience.

Out of Your Depth

The scale of bad news will vary. Where the news is something that you have no experience in or think is out of your field, you may consult with an expert. For example, a presentation to teenagers about drugs would probably be better dealt with by a doctor, psychologist or counsellor. However, if they are not actually involved directly in the issue you should not delegate the entire responsibility for the presentation to the expert. If you have called them in to provide expert advice, they should follow from your introduction.

For example, you might begin by explaining to students the reasons you are concerned about their exposure to drugs. You might include a story about an anonymous person you know who has lost a friend or family member through a drug addiction that started out harmlessly enough, but soon became more serious. After explaining why you are concerned for them, you could introduce the expert by saying, "Dr Bob Smith has joined us today because he specialises in treating people for drug addiction. He chose this career when he was 25, after seeing one of his friends lose a battle with drug addiction. I have asked him to speak to us today from both a personal and medical perspective. Please make him welcome."

In a sensitive situation where people will be deeply affected by the news, it might be better to let people absorb bad news before bringing in experts and action plans. If your audience is hearing the news for the first time, they will need time to accept what has happened, before they can hear solutions. If there are no solutions or positive points, the bad news should be a sharing process. People will want to think about the issue in their own time and talk about how they feel.

The Formula

Announcing bad news requires discretion and sensitivity. As with every presentation you give, it will vary depending on your message and your audience. However, the basic formula for delivering bad news is:

1. Warn the audience that you have bad news.
2. Announce the bad news.
3. Identify with the audience.
4. Emphasise any positive points.
5. Create an action plan.

Warn the audience that you have bad news. Begin by warning your audience that you are about to share some bad news with them. This way they will be able to prepare themselves for what you are about to say. It will ease some of the shock if they are mentally primed.

Announce the bad news. For example, "The bad news is that this year's staff bonuses have been cancelled". Having heard this, the audience will probably be angry.

Identify with the audience. Make a statement that empathises with the audience. For example, "I am sure that some of you are very angry and upset at this decision." Or "some of you will disagree with the decision."

Typically you cannot change the decision. So, be **firm** that the decision cannot be changed, but **flexible** about dealing with the consequences. If people are in shock or denial, you may need to patiently and calmly repeat the message several times. It helps to have a written announcement for people to take away and read, after recovering from the shock.

One method of calming an upset audience is to summarise your perception of what the audience feels. For example, "Clearly, you are angry and upset and you think there are too many redundancies. I do not necessarily agree with you but I do understand what you are saying." If they agree with your summary, then you can move on, if not ask them to tell you what you missed and then try to summarise and get agreement again.

There may be a risk of people using your words in legal actions, so make clear that you are trying to understand their opinions and that you do not necessarily agree with them. As insurance to protect themselves, some presenters will make notes of the meeting afterwards. Others might ensure there is a neutral witness in the room.

Emphasise any positive points. Follow up with something to appease their anger. Do not make up an excuse, but try to emphasise any encouraging aspects of the message. For instance, "While these redundancies are not good news, if the hard decision had been delayed, more people would have lost their jobs. For the people who are staying, the company will be more competitive and your jobs will be more secure."

Create an action plan. Once the audience has digested the bad news you may like to propose an action plan for dealing with the events. Guide the audience through what you or an expert on the issue recommends as the best course of action. Or, where applicable, offer some alternatives. For example, "We want to help you all as much as possible. So we have contacted an industry recruiter. The recruiter will be conducting interviews next week and hopefully will be able to find new jobs for most of you. We have also arranged for two secretaries to format new resumes for you. Additionally, we will have a counsellor on site for the next three days and we encourage you to talk to him." Providing an action plan may help people focus on solutions.

DELIVERING BAD NEWS TOOL: INFORMING FARMERS ABOUT SOIL DEGRADATION

How will you warn the audience that you have bad news?	My audience consists of members of my local farming community who are concerned about the growing media revelations about soil degradation. The bad news is that they will no longer be able to grow food. The advertisements for the presentation will indicate that the presentation will be on a topic of serious environmental concern around food scarcity. It will also indicate that there is positive news and ways people can help.
How will you word the negative message?	I will start by pouring a handful of dirt into a bucket and say the dirt is dead. I will have another bucket full of dirt and worms. I will allow this to drop from my hand into the bucket. I will then start the discussion around the dead dirt.
How do you intend to identify with the audience?	Draw on the similarity of our peril, given that I have seen top soil disappear during floods. I will show some pictures of my farm and the damage caused by these events.
What is your strategy for diffusing audience anger?	I plan to reiterate all of the evidence that shows the degrading abilities of these floods and offer the solution of Permaculture. I will be careful not to use complicated scientific jargon, which would alienate the audience and make them feel like they do not know enough to be able to participate in the solution.
What are some positive aspects of the message?	We have a good idea of where the problem is coming from. If we act now, we can minimise the harm to the environment. There are alternative farming methods that will allow your farm to grow in a sustainable, chemical free, organic way. Permaculture has the knowledge and the information necessary to be able to financially sustain you whilst being environmentally friendly.
What action plan will you propose for dealing with the bad event?	After giving my presentation, I will circulate a form, collecting contact details (email addresses in particular) of people who wish to access more information and tools on Permaculture. When I contact the group I will give them the dates and times of local Permaculture meetings and invite them to my farm to see the radical difference of a chemical free property.
Will you consult with someone else regarding this issue?	I will access pictures from other permaculturalist's that have evidence of the benefits of using swales to control water flow.
Would the news be better delivered from someone else, and if so, who?	I am passionate about this topic and committed to mobilising people to do something about it. With the help of some scientists and lobbyists, and good presenting skills, I think I will be a good person to get the ball rolling.

Insight 36
Music and Sound

*"Between stimulus and response,
people have the freedom to choose."*

Stephen Covey

What is the most frightening horror movie you have seen? What is the most romantic love story you have ever watched? Would either of these movies have been as effective without their soundtrack? Music is potentially one of the most effective elements of a presentation. It is also the element that is overlooked most often.

Sound is one of our earliest sensations and throughout life it remains a powerful tool when Persuading For Results. It can create a mood, highlight key points and grab attention. Music has been shown to increase learning, and as many students will testify, music makes monotonous tasks more interesting.

For an early morning presentation, you might play some up-beat music as people enter the room, to help wake them up. Music is also an effective way of taking the awkwardness out of a coffee break, or for creating a relaxed or fun atmosphere. If your audience is made up of people in the same age group, play some songs that were popular when they were teenagers.

Some ways to use music in a presentation are:	Play music as people enter the room.
	Play music during coffee breaks.
	Play soft background music during small group work. Playing music during group work helps create an informal atmosphere, which is conductive to spontaneous and creative interpersonal interaction. Songs without lyrics are less distracting.
	Play music as a signal that small groups are required to reassemble as a large group.
	Play music to signal and celebrate a successful outcome.
	Play a fanfare for the introduction of a guest speaker.
	Play music for relaxation or exercise time.
	Play music during visualisation exercises.
	Play music at the conclusion of the session to give a professional and positive parting impression.

While people do not often think to incorporate music into their presentation, they do often use computer generated sound to punctuate their PowerPoint® presentations. See *Insight 45—Death by PowerPoint®*.

Do not break the law

Music is powerful in presentations. However, be careful not to infringe copyright in the country where you are presenting. In Australia each year we pay for the right to play music in meetings and when we deliver keynote addresses at conferences.

Style—Delivering Your Persuasion

"There are three things in this world that are hard to do:
One, climb a fence that leans towards you;
Two, kiss a girl that leans away from you;
Three, try to help someone who won't help themself."
Peter Sullivan

Insight 37
Dealing with Nervousness

*"If you can keep your head when all about you are losing theirs,
it's just possible you haven't grasped the situation."*

Jean Kerr — Humorist

Even professional speakers will sometimes be nervous. Renowned as a great speaker, Mark Twain once said, "There are two types of speakers: Those that are nervous and those that are liars." The good news is that you can make nervous energy work for you, not against you.

Audience Reaction

There are two common responses to a nervous presentation. The audience will feel sympathetic towards the presenter or the audience will feel embarrassed. The usual pattern is sympathy for the first few minutes, then embarrassment.

The audience will stare at the nervous presenter, noticing a choked or squeaky voice, a red face, a nervous twitch, hyperactive pacing or a death grip on the lectern. They will hear the nervous tremor in repeated phrases such as 'you know what I mean?' or 'okay?' They will start to squirm with you. They may give the presenter their sympathy, but they will withhold their respect.

You probably will not display *all the* above symptoms, but even a few can ruin a presentation. The good news is that you can control your emotions and nervous reactions.

Change Your Thought Patterns

What are people afraid of?

- Failure
- Humiliation
- Losing people's attention or respect
- Forgetting

If you concentrate on bad things that could happen during your presentation, you are likely to let your fears escalate and you may go out in front of your audience with a self-defeating attitude. You need to identify your fears and use positive self-talk—'what if I fail' should be replaced by 'when I succeed'.

You can build your mental toughness and your resilience using some practical tools. We have found helpful and practical: Martin Seligmann's book, *Learned Optimism* (2006), Karen Reivich & Andrew Shatté's, *The Resilience Factor* (2002) and Sarah Edelman's book, *Change Your Thinking* (2006).

In summary, be in control of your subject matter, technology and audience. Control is the key. Shift the focus away from yourself and onto your message.

Practice Makes Perfect

People respond to nervousness in different ways. You need to identify your own nervous habits and start to manage them. This might mean spending time practising smooth hand movements instead of jerky twitches, learning breath control, and taking deep breaths instead of coming out with nervous phrases. It is also a good idea to steer clear of caffeinated drinks before your presentation, as they will just make you jittery.

Finally, the two most important parts of your presentation are the close and the opening and you cannot afford to have those stages undermined by nerves. So, we recommend you memorise the first and last three minutes of your presentation.

The Audience Wants You to Succeed

Keep in mind the audience is not the enemy. The audience wants you to succeed—for their own sake.

Using Humour

"Life is either a daring adventure or nothing."

Helen Keller

What is humour? It can be many things—a light touch, rueful or ironic statements, a quick joke, or an amusing anecdote. For most speakers, humorous anecdotes, especially told against themselves, work well. No doubt you are familiar with the story that starts with a rueful 'You will never guess what happened to me...'

Playing with Expectations

A television program on men's health showed a presenter winning an audience over with the following anecdote with a wry twist, "My father died before he was fifty. He was mowing the lawn, and he had a heart attack. I learnt a powerful lesson from that. I've never mowed the lawn since."

The humour comes from the element of surprise. The audience expects to hear an earnest story about taking better care of one's health, getting fit, de-stressing, and the genetic likelihood of the speaker having a heart attack at a relatively young age, like his father. Surprisingly, the 'wrong' element is picked out giving the presentation a lighter feel.

Humour lies in the unexpected and has its roots in empathy. When used properly, humour will promote an air of familiarity and intimacy between you and your audience.

The Benefits of Laughing

Studies show that laughing increases the immune system's activity, decreases stress and improves the respiratory tract. In addition, laughing uses both sides of the brain, promoting creativity and problem solving.

Humour achieves:

- A connection between you and the audience.
- Rapport—people love to laugh. If you can make them laugh, they will like you.
- Release of tension—after a serious part of the presentation or a long session, laughter can reduce stress.
- Increased energy.

Be Wary of Humour

Despite all of its benefits, in general we recommend that you avoid formal jokes. Funny anecdotes are much easier to deliver and are more likely to succeed. Jokes need excellent timing and pacing and an audience in tune with the presenter's brand of humour—a combination that is rare.

If you decide to use jokes in your presentation, make sure your jokes are appropriate. There are two distinct types of humour—negative and positive. Negative humour preys on a victim, highlighting the differences between people. This humour is often at someone else's expense, spreading ignorance and prejudice. Such humour risks offending your audience.

We recently attended a farewell function for a colleague who was about to leave Australia to live in the United States of America. Some people stepped up to the microphone to say a few words.

As we listened, one speaker started by providing a 'roasting' of people in the USA. At first, this light-hearted roasting added some humour to the speaker's presentation. The problem was, this 'humour' continued for ten minutes, until we wanted to find a hole to crawl into in case there was an American in the room.

Positive Humour

Positive humour is about sharing experiences. It draws on our common ground, our frustrations and successes. This humour encourages understanding between people, as we laugh at ourselves rather than at each other. Think of the popular comedians in your part of the world. Those very funny men and women have entire repertoires that are about our everyday common experiences. Humour is best when recounting a personal experience. Try to connect the joke to yourself or someone you know.

We believe humour can energise and persuade. We recommend using positive humour during presentations and, where possible, avoiding formal jokes, in favour of funny anecdotes.

Insight 39
Managing Problem Participants

*"The role of a teacher is to give our kids the tools to think,
not to tell them what to think."*

Jack Mackay

Sometimes when you are presenting you will have to deal with problem audience members. Remain polite and courteous despite how you may wish to respond. Be aware that disruptive behaviour is a symptom of an audience member's needs. It is usually part of an attempt to gain attention, acknowledgement, acceptance, stimulation or something else. The key is to stay in control.

Typically, problem audience members fall into one of the following broad categories:

- The Interrupter
- The Heckler
- The Unfriendly
- The Disruptor
- The Dominator

The Interrupter

Almost every group has an interrupter. The interrupter will annoy you, disrupt the group dynamics and might make your persuasion less effective. Even so, when you face an interrupter ask yourself, "Are they interrupting because my message is not clear enough?" If your message does seem clear and comprehensive and the interruptions are unnecessary you must manage that audience member.

The constant interrupter can be dealt with by firmly expressed phrases such as "Thank you for that comment. Now I would like to hear from someone who has not already contributed." Or, "I will stop for feedback and discussion at the end of each topic. Please hold your questions, so we can deal with them properly then."

If the interruption is irrelevant to the purpose of your persuasion, you may respond with, "That is an *interesting* comment but it is not relevant to today's presentation, so why don't you stay back after the presentation and we can talk about it." Few people will take you up on that suggestion. The constant interrupter usually just wants an opportunity to dominate or seize the attention of the group.

The Heckler

Often the heckler is trying to alleviate boredom. The audience may be lacking interaction and stimulation, and the heckler is trying to add some excitement by frustrating you or trying to be funny.

Be careful not to become too defensive. This will only escalate the situation. First, analyse your own behaviour and see if the problem is with your presentation. One common cause of heckling is a slow-moving presentation.

Try to ignore hecklers. If the heckler sees you are not perturbed by their comments, they may give up. Sometimes body language can help. Moving closer to the heckler without necessarily focusing your attention on them may stop them.

If the heckler continues, you can try to incorporate them into the presentation by asking the audience a question, and then singling them out for an answer. Often the heckler will want to remain anonymous, so ask them to state their name and company before they answer.

If all else fails, confront the heckler. In this situation, stop your presentation and talk to the heckler privately. Listen to their complaint and then ask for their co-operation.

The Unfriendly

If the audience is particularly unfriendly, try to highlight any points of agreement you have with them. Do not be lured into an argument.

Consider reasons your audience is reacting negatively. Is your message contrary to their ideas? Are they bored? Do they believe that you lack credibility? Whatever the reason, you may need to address it either directly or in a more subtle way. Sometimes just acknowledging the problem can reduce the tension. For instance, you might say, "I realise you are already familiar with doing your tax returns, and many of you are well aware of the benefits you can claim. I know this might seem like a dry or boring topic, but with this latest software, you may soon realise that you are entitled to many more tax savings."

Try some of the techniques from *Insight 27—Involve your audience.* These break down barriers and release tension.

The Disruptor

If people arrive late or leave early, try to ignore them. Do not take it personally, because they may have a genuine reason for arriving late or needing to leave. Do not waste everyone else's time by stopping the presentation.

There are a few ways to deal with people talking during your presentation. In a large group it is best just to ignore them. For a smaller group, make eye contact with the talkers. You may have to stop speaking until they look up and get the message. If this does not work, ask them to take their conversation elsewhere or ask them to wait until later.

If there is a conflict within the audience, send the message that you are the one in control. Defuse tension by reassuring that everyone will get a turn to speak.

The Dominator

If someone is dominating an open discussion or activity, then you will need to take control so others have a chance to contribute. Ask other people in the group for their input. You may even have to say something like, "Does anyone have any comments, besides Susan?"

If an audience member is rambling, do not be afraid to cut in and summarise the rambler's comments. Ask others for their opinions. The audience will be relieved that they don't have to listen to the rambler.

Just remember that no matter what distress an audience member might be causing, you are the one in control. It is up to you to deal with problems so your entire presentation is not compromised due to one audience member who thinks they know more about the topic than you do.

Insight 40
Location

*"Two roads diverged in a yellow wood ...
And I took the one less travelled by,
And that has made all the difference."*

Robert Frost

The three most important considerations when buying property are location, location, location. When persuading for results, location is an important factor to consider as it has a big influence on the mood and outcome. Many companies schedule their annual conferences at holiday spots, to set a relaxed tone for the proceedings. However, more often the major decision is the location and size of the room, not which tropical island to fly your audience to.

Location

The choice of location will often be simple, "Your place or mine?" When you do have a choice about presenting in a different location, consider convenience and cost. Using a laptop or iPad improves your options. You might like to present over a meal at a restaurant or on an aeroplane, provided you are seated next to your one-person audience. However, for most presentations, your most important consideration will be the size and set up of an indoor location.

Size does matter

Size does matter. When assessing the suitability of a room to present in, first it should hold your audience comfortably. If you are using a data projector screen, the screen must be far enough away from the audience so they can see the entire screen comfortably. Sometimes, you will need to have extra space for activities or for tables so the audience can take notes. Think about whether you want additional rooms so you can break into group work.

People do not like cramped conditions. A sign of an inappropriate set-up is people balancing their belongings on their laps. Also, if people cannot cross their legs without disturbing the person in front of them, the room is too small.

Just as it is important to have enough room, it is also problematic to have a small audience in a large room. This can make audience members feel lost, insignificant, and afraid to contribute to group discussions.

To ensure you get the right size of room, book your presentation well ahead. Consider rescheduling or booking an outside room if you can not get the room size you want.

Temperature

The only thing worse than freezing your way through a presentation, is sweating your way through; a warm room will encourage people to drift off to sleep. It is usually better to err towards a cooler room.

Ventilation

Adequate ventilation is important. In most cultures it will be inappropriate to allow people to smoke during a presentation.

Lighting

Poor lighting will frustrate even the most enthusiastic note taker. It will also encourage the audience to drift off to sleep. Regardless of how many visuals you use during a presentation, do not conduct the entire presentation in darkness. If you plan to keep one slide on for a few minutes of explanation, turn the lights back on.

Distractions

Make sure the room is free from distractions such as phone calls, staff problems and people-traffic. Arrange for messages to be held until the end the presentation. Remind people to switch off mobile phones.

LOCATION TOOL: COLOSSAL SPORTS

Location	Executive Board Room, Sydney office.
Size	15 square metres.
Temperature	22° C.
Ventilation	Good.
Lighting	Good.
Distractions	Will keep door closed to block out office noise and arrange to have telephone messages recorded. No telephones or mobiles inside the room.
Contact for equipment problems	Janine extension 948.
Emergency phone	Phone 000.

LOCATION TOOL: COMMUNITY GARDEN

Location	Council chambers boardroom
Size	5 × 5 metres
Temperature	24 degrees
Ventilation	Air conditioning
Lighting	Fluorescent
Distractions	None
Contact for equipment problems	Ms Hannah Armstrong 02 9498 4563
Emergency phone	000

Insight 41
Room Layout

"Give me somewhere to stand, and I will move the earth."
Archimedes, 287–212BC.

When persuading for results, having selected an appropriate room and confirmed the size of your audience, it is important to think about room layout. Let's explore some of the options.

Theatre Style

A theatre style layout is appropriate for presentations involving a large audience. Each audience member has a clear view of the screen, especially if the seating is tiered. If possible, arrange seats in a semicircle, so people on the fringe seats do not feel isolated from the rest of the group. This also prevents people getting stiff necks from craning to see the screen.

There are two drawbacks to this arrangement. First, the theatre style does not encourage discussion. Secondly, unless the audience has individual fold-up desks, people find it difficult to take notes.

U-Shape

For presentations where you wish to encourage participation, discussion and note taking, a U-shape is better. The U-shape arrangement is most effective for groups with less than fifteen people. In larger rooms, one U-shape can be included inside another.

The best way to position your guests is with the key decision makers in the seats opposite you, at the base of the U. Position people you want input or consensus from to your left. Reserve the seats to your right for your staff or for people who will not contribute to discussion. Your attention will be constantly divided between the power brokers and the contributors, and the people on the right will not enjoy much of your eye contact. Some presenters chose to mix people around. This might be irritating for the decision makers who wish to confer at various times throughout the meeting. Having organised seating will help you manage the audience.

Boardroom style

The boardroom style is very similar to the U-shape. The main difference is a boardroom style makes it easier to pass papers across the table. This style is often the only option, as many meeting rooms are equipped with one large rectangular table.

Cabaret Style

The cabaret style immediately suggests discussion, interaction, small group work and food. It is a good option for a lunchtime address at a conference, or for a long meeting, when refreshments will be brought in periodically. If you use this arrangement, capitalize on the benefits of having ready-made small groups. Encourage discussion, interaction and teamwork.

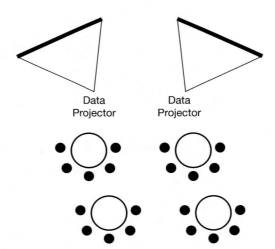

It is useful to have two screens, one screen to outline your main conclusions and the other screen to show statistics and more detailed data to support those conclusions. This is particularly useful when there are two presenters presenting at the same time. The stereo screen arrangement can be adapted to the cabaret (or almost any other arrangement) to allow a dual visual presentation.

Classroom Style

The classroom set-up works well for large groups and long sessions. It allows all the audience to see the screen and provides a table for them to lean on when taking notes. The tables can form small discussion groups, although when tables are too long, interaction is awkward.

Round Table

In the tradition of King Arthur's Knights of the Round Table, the round table promotes a lively exchange of ideas, under conditions of equality. In this arrangement nobody occupies a dominant position. All ideas are welcome, all people are equal. The drawback of this arrangement is that you, as the presenter, may have difficultly keeping the discussion centred on your agenda.

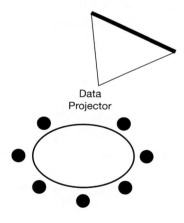

Data Projector

Insight 42
Facilities

*"Whenever you see a successful business,
someone once made a courageous decision."*

Peter Drucker

When persuading for results, we frequently talk about how to get your audience to believe you. By telling the next story, we risk undermining our own credibility, because the next story is hard to believe. It is a true story about a recent presentation that we attended. If you are serious about persuading for results and this story does not convince you of the importance of checking facilities and equipment, nothing will. In an age with wireless microphones, Broadway-style lighting facilities, ergonomic conference chairs and every other luxury imaginable, some readers might think the following story had sprung from our imaginations. We wish it had.

A Presentation to Remember?

We recently attended a high profile presentation at a large firm. The Master of Ceremonies (MC) gave a fabulous introduction from the left of the stage and invited the guest speaker to step onto the platform to speak. The podium was at the right of the stage. Unfortunately, the lights had only been set up to shine on the MC on the left, and the guest speaker's podium was in the darkness.

For several minutes people played with light switches, creating a disco atmosphere. The lights could not be redirected, so two people stepped up to help move the podium to the left of the stage, into the light. Satisfied that everything was in order, the guest speaker started to speak. Unfortunately, during relocating the podium, the microphone had stopped working.

After several minutes someone produced a cordless microphone and it seemed that everything would be okay. Except the microphone did not work. Eventually, the MC offered to share his lapel microphone. He asked questions and the guest leaned in to the MC's chest to answer them. Unfortunately, the MC was very short and the guest speaker was very tall. The guest did not look particularly distinguished bent in half, tucked under the MC's chin like a baby penguin.

The audience members shuffled awkwardly, but we were not sure whether they felt embarrassed for the guest, or whether they were simply uncomfortable standing for two hours at the end of a long day. Fortunately, there was food and wine, but because it did not appear until the presentation began, there was a constant murmur of "would you like some wine" and "yes please".

Most people managed without seats, but we were a bit nervous for the elderly woman with two walking sticks, who kept shifting uncomfortably from leg to leg. We need not have worried about her, because in the end it was a man who collapsed, pulling down two of the large banners on his way to the floor.

At that stage I think the MC realised that it was time to wind things up. He did so by imploring the audience to, 'please, please go down to the back of the room and buy our products. You can get a great new product for $200. That is, $25 for the product and $175 as a donation to our company!"

We can not tell you what happened next, because we, with many others, quietly slipped out the back door.

Nothing we say can prepare you for every contingency, as we do not know what facilities you will use. However, you should check the availability and operation of the following, at the very least.

Equipment
- A data projector
- Flip charts/easel
- A screen
- Other audio-visual aids
- A whiteboard
- Extra paper for flip charts
- A computer and screen
- Working white board/flip-chart pens

Room
- Is the room well-ventilated, presentable and comfortable?
- Does the room have wireless internet, power outlets and other facilities for the laptops and modems of audience members? (Are these designed to avoid being trip hazards?)
- Does the room have all the equipment you need?
- Is it possible to hire the equipment you need and to bring it to the meeting room?
- Do you need a microphone to be heard?
- Is the image from the data projector clear?
- Is the room relatively free from distractions and noise? Consider traffic, telephones, and activities in adjoining rooms.
- If the discussion is confidential, is it possible to hear the discussion from outside the room?
- Is the room well lit? Can lighting be dimmed or only turned off completely?
- Is the room close to the bathroom?
- Are there facilities for making coffee, tea and serving refreshments?
- Do you have the phone number of someone you can call if there is a problem with the room or equipment?

FACILITIES TOOL: COLOSSAL SPORTS

Stereo or mono (two or one projectors?)	Mono (one).
Theatre	
U-shape	
Boardroom	Will be using this style, as it is the only option in the room. However, it will help promote a comfortable environment that the audience is already familiar with.
Cabaret	
Classroom	
Where are extra paper and pens	Not applicable.

FACILITIES TOOL: COMMUNITY GARDEN

Stereo or mono (two or one projectors?)	One data projector
Theatre	No
U-shape	No
Boardroom	yes
Cabaret	No
Classroom	No
Where are extra paper and pens	I will bring extra in my basket

Insight 43
Coffee Breaks and Meal Breaks

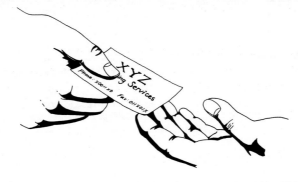

"Referral business comes from what you get that you don't pay for, not what you get that you pay for!"

Martin Grunstein

Much business persuasion is conducted in social settings, reaching agreement over a meal, a round of golf, or a few cocktails. Similarly, business relationships can be consolidated during 'time out' periods in presentations—such as coffee breaks or meal breaks.

In longer presentations, it is good to stop for a coffee break so people can refresh themselves, but also, so they can mingle. Your task during the break should not be to pour coffee unless you wish to use this as an icebreaker. Instead, when persuading for results you should seek out the movers and shakers of the meeting, talking to key audience members and gaining vital feedback.

If some of the audience seem to be resisting your ideas, some presenters ensure they chat to these people at the break to try to understand their concerns better. Sometimes it is possible to resolve the concerns during the break. However more often, in case other audience members share the same concerns, the persuasive presenter will try to address their concerns in subsequent sessions of the presentation.

To ensure the coffee break runs smoothly, make sure all necessary preparations have been made. Have someone else look after tasks such as preparing the coffee, making sure there is food available and ensuring there is milk and sugar. Just a quick tip, if it is an important presentation, make sure the food is good, the refreshments enjoyable and the coffee fresh.

As we have discussed throughout the book, your role is to influence and to persuade in a group and one-on-one. Influencing during coffee and meal breaks is critical because it improves the credibility of your message.

Before the presentation, consider who you need to talk to during the break. Also consider how you will open the conversation, what topics you will broach and what information you need. Know which audience members you wish to introduce to each other.

The danger of the coffee break is you might get trapped talking to the less important people. This might sound heartless, but talking to a company junior about the traffic is not the most effective way to use your time to persuade for results.

Be prepared to politely excuse yourself with the words, "It is wonderful to meet you and I hope you enjoy the second half of the presentation. Will you excuse me while I go and see how the other participants are?" This is an acceptable way to excuse yourself.

Food can be a powerful tool of persuasion. When people are sharing food, they relax, are less aggressive and less prone to conflict. Sometimes arranging a lunch meeting can help persuade people to work together more constructively on difficult issues. We suggest sandwiches because the pace of eating is slower, whereas eating hot food needs more concentration and sets a faster pace.

For a difficult topic, a useful method of persuasion is to arrange for the sandwiches to be ready before the presentation. Encourage the participants to start eating, and then begin your presentation. People won't be able to interrupt you while they are eating, so you will be assured of at least a few minutes of peace. For this to be effective, keep your presentation short and allow plenty of time for discussions before the food is finished.

Cialdini in his book *Influence*, explains that food helps persuade people because your ideas are associated with a good feeling from eating. Cialdini writes:

"Using what he (Razran) terms the 'luncheon technique', he explains people become fonder of people and things they experienced while they were eating. In the example most relevant for our purposes (Razran, 1940), subjects were presented with some political statements they had rated once before. At the end of the experiment, after all the political statements had been presented, Razran found that only certain ones of them had gained in approval—those that had been shown while the food was being eaten. These changes in liking seemed to have occurred unconsciously, since the subjects could not remember which of the statements they had seen while the food was being served."

Cialdini explains this understanding comes from the work Pavlov did with dogs. Remember Pavlov rang a bell while dogs were eating and the dogs became so conditioned that when Pavlov rang the bell with no food, the dogs salivated.

Razran found there are many normal responses to food besides salivation. One response is a good and favourable feeling. This positive attitude can transfer to anything that is closely associated with good food.

Section 5
Persuasion on the Run

"The really nice thing about not planning is that failure comes as a complete surprise. And is not preceded by a period of worry and depression."

Insight 44
Preparing with a Laptop

"We provide prompt service, when we have time!"

Mr. Foo — Singapore

At airports throughout the world, we see passengers travelling with their laptops. Security officers examine laptops, businesspeople connect to the Internet in airport lounges and managers put the final touches on reports while cruising at 30,000 feet.

The laptop is an indispensable tool of business because it serves as a compact, convenient and portable office. For the persuader, its value reaches far beyond a simple PC. It allows the persuader to deliver dynamic and powerful presentations outside the office with relatively little trouble. More importantly, it allows the persuader to customise presentations for different audiences quickly.

Buying a Laptop

Computer technology changes so fast that it is difficult to advise on what laptop to buy. However, we can say that by investing in a good quality laptop, you will be able to work exclusively from that laptop, even when in your own office. This may save you from some of the problems that occur with low quality models. The added benefit of working mainly from the laptop, even while in the office, is that you are less likely to run into the problem that you have left essential data on your PC.

Before buying a laptop, think hard about how you plan to use it. There are two broad laptop categories. The first consists of light, thin laptops, which are intended for people who carry their laptops with them much of the time. These models are convenient for a presenter who uses a laptop frequently, and particularly useful for people who carry their laptops with them as they travel by aeroplane. The disadvantage of these thin, light models is that they may not have all accessories integrated into the laptop. Instead, some accessories, such as an external disk drive, must be connected externally. Also, a 'thin' laptop is usually more expensive than a 'thick' one.

The second category of laptop is marketed towards those who want the performance of a desktop PC, with the option to occasionally use the laptop on the go. Such models have almost all accessories built in, but as you are hurrying between airport gates or jumping in and out of taxis, you will start to feel the extra weight.

Regardless of which laptop you buy, be sure that it includes all the features you think you will need. Think about processor speed, hard drive, RAM, sound and video cards and any other features. Upgrading a laptop can be expensive, so it is better to choose carefully. Sophisticated presentations use lots of memory, both hard drive and RAM. The trend is for presentation programs to use more and more memory and we suggest that you spend a little more on computer memory. At the time of writing 512 MB of RAM and a Pentium chip should run many sophisticated presentations. However hardware and software are changing rapidly. If you intend to use advanced features, sound, pictures and video in your presentation, seek technical advice about which laptop will suit your needs. If you can, test the laptop with a typical presentation. Just remember that when a computer is new the hard disk is not filled with data and so it will run faster than normal.

Preparing with a laptop

When preparing with a laptop, the first thing to think about is the message you want to convey. It is important to use technology to communicate your message, not use your message as an opportunity to show off your technology. Technology is only ever there to help deliver your message. Therefore everything you do, every graphic and every sound must have a purpose in the delivery of your message.

Using an iPad

When using an iPad most of the information for laptops applies, just ensure that you can make changes to your presentation on the run and practice before hand to ensure a smooth and persuasive presentation; this is further discussed in Insight 46.

Insight 45
Death By PowerPoint®

*"He who is good with a hammer tends
to think everything is a nail."*

Abraham Maslow

We do not remember where we first heard the phrase Death by PowerPoint®. However, it captures perfectly the feeling you have when a presenter has text and slides flying in from all directions with a different sound accompanying each addition. It also describes the frustration when a presenter has so many words on a slide that you cannot finish reading before they change to the next slide.

PowerPoint® is a great tool, but PowerPoint® is only as effective as the person driving it. We have created and seen hundreds of presentations and suggest three rules:

Keep it simple

- Keep the structure simple
- Keep each slide simple
- Use effects rarely and only for impact

PowerPoint® is only a tool!
What's your message?

Keep the structure simple

First ensure you have a structure, see *Insight 17—Structure Your Content*. Regularly we see many presentations where there is just one slide after another, soon the audience has no idea where the presenter is going or where they have been. Often in the middle of the presentation the audience wonders, "What's the point of this slide?" Confusing an audience will not help persuade them. So, choose a structure and then use signposts.

When you drive from one place to another, how do you know where you are? At regular intervals, there are signposts showing the distance from your departure and the distance to your destination. On international flights they often have a video display that shows similar information. The simplest way to signpost is to use an agenda slide at the beginning of the presentation and repeat it at the beginning of each section with the section title highlighted.

Agenda

- Why listen
- Keep the structure simple
  - Put in a structure
  - Use signposts
- Keep each slide simple
  - Good use of fonts helps
  - Use less words to encourage listening
- Use effects rarely and only for impact
- Conclusions

For experienced PowerPoint® users, an advanced method is useful for complex presentations or presentations where you may wish to show only parts of a large presentation to different audiences. We suggest using an agenda with custom shows for each of the main sections. This is simply a single agenda slide with a hyperlink on each main heading. Clicking on the hyperlink starts a custom show. If you have set up the link correctly, when the show finishes the presentation returns to the original agenda slide and the hyperlink changes colour to show that you have viewed that topic.

To set up a custom show, look at the menu under *Slide show—Custom Shows*. Remember that when you create the shows, you should tick the box for *Show and*

Return. Also, in the slide sorter view hide all the slides except for the agenda slide. The first time you use this technique it may seem to be unnecessary effort, however the feedback from the audience about how professional the presentation looks will soon convince you the effort is worthwhile.

Keep each slide simple

One aspect of simplicity is creating slides with as few words as possible and making sure the words you do include have a clear font. Fonts are partly a personal preference and some presenters will not suggest a font. However, we use the guidance of the publishers of books and newspapers who typically use two fonts, one for headings and one for text. We recommend a sans serif font for the slide titles and a serif font for the text.

The serif fonts such as Times Roman or Garamond are easier to read than a sans serif font like Arial. That is why most of the books and newspapers use these fonts for their text. Books and newspapers use a sans serif font for headlines—their key message. We recommend sans serif for the titles of slides because that is where your message should be for each slide.

One way to keep each slide simple is to use the Format-slide layout command to choose a new slide. Here you will find different slide layouts, and if you always use these then your presentation will have a consistent look. Sometimes in a presentation the position of bullet points on a slide change from slide to slide. The human brain is conditioned to look for small differences and some of the audience will wonder why these bullets are in the centre of the screen while the last ones were on the left. If they are wondering, they are not listening to you.

Having discussed the use of fonts we now move on to using fewer words to encourage listening. Jerry Weissman was a television producer before he began to teach companies how to present to raise millions of dollars from the US stock market. In his book Presenting to Win, he sums up this idea elegantly as a working principle 'Less Is More' and argues that PowerPoint® is a support for the presenter and not a substitute. If a presenter puts all the words they will say into the slides, why does the audience need the presenter? For maximum impact:

- Limit to 5 main points per slide, but never more than 7
- 1 message on each slide
- 1 message on each chart

Using fewer words is more powerful and one way to do this is to use more visuals, see Insights 22, 23, 24, 25 and 26. Pictures, diagrams and charts all help to use fewer words. Another method is to use a GIF image—a moving picture. These are commonly seen on websites. We first saw this used elegantly in a presentation to bring a complex chart to life, showing how the intersection of two lines changed with changing conditions as both lines moved simultaneously. The GIF enabled the presenter to make a complex idea seem simple. The audience could see the complex interaction on one slide rather than having to remember a series of previous slides. To use a GIF, presenters need PowerPoint® 2000 or later versions and a program like Paintshop Pro with Animation Shop to create a GIF.

Use effects rarely and only for impact

There are many possible visual and sound effects. Our recommendation is to use effects rarely and only when they increase the impact of the slide. Remember, visual and sound effects can irritate the audience. Variation for emphasis can come from graphics and colour—it need not come from the effects.

There are three kinds of effects: slide transitions, text transitions and sounds. For slide transitions we recommend using *None* because the audience will focus on the effect for the brief duration of each slide transition. With no slide transition, we suggest that the impact of the next slide is higher and the presentation has more 'punch'. Sometimes fading to black between major sections of the presentation helps signal to your audience a new topic, but in general, subtlety and consistency are best.

For most text transitions use *appear* or *dissolve*. Many people never change the default, which is *fly-in from left*. Watching slide after slide of text flying in from the left again and again becomes very irritating. Similarly, bombarding your audience with zooming graphics, screens that fade in and out and bullet points emerging from all points of the slide can detract from your message rather than strengthen it. When using bullet points, to list complex or controversial points, consider revealing the points one at a time. If each point is simple, reveal them all immediately. Revealing points one at a time builds suspense; if the next point is trivial or obvious, some of the audience will be disappointed.

The *wipe* effect can be effective to build pictures or charts. Choosing to *wipe* left or right, up or down directs the audience's attention in the same direction. When combined with the option to disappear after display, this effect is useful for gradually building graphics or charts.

Finally, we recommend using sounds only occasionally and when they have an impact. For example, a cash register sound for a key figure can sometimes add impact. If you use sounds, we suggest use no more than one per presentation and that you use quality speakers, that project a good sound all the audience can hear. Using too many sounds, may give the audience a headache. Remember, a symphony is a beautiful collection of sounds organised by a professional, a cacophony is a terrible collection of sounds organised by an amateur.

Use less bullets

When using PowerPoint®, it is tempting (and easy) to produce slide after slide of text, full of bullet points. It is seductively easy to add a slide using the template with bullet points. However, using only bullet points can bore the audience and can get in the way of your message. Andrew Abela, *Advanced Presentation By Design: creating communication that drives action* (2008), quotes some research that suggests, "Projecting slides with text bullet points and/or irrelevant graphics such as clip art during your presentation will likely have worse results than speaking without any visual aids at all." (p90)

Two ways to use less bullets points are to use words in tables and use words in text boxes. Words in tables (WiT) was popularised by Jon Moon, in his excellent book, *How to make an IMPACT: Influence, inform and impress with your reports, presentations, business documents, charts and graphs* (2009). In brief, he shows how removing bullets can make your message clearer and show the message structure and can make your message stand out. From the book, contrast the same information in bullets and in a table. For us, the table is more persuasive.

Why choose us?

- Being the biggest, we get you the best deal from our market leverage
- Our clever web system gives you 24/7 access
- Because of our strong parent company, you get the security of dealing with a strong and stable financial company
- Having won The Employer of Choice last month, you get highly motivated and productive employees working on your projects
- We have been serving clients for 150 years, so you get cost effective and proven methods
- Your case is presented not by a salesman, but by one of our accounts executives, so you get people who understand your business, not just understand their products

Why choose us?

Feature	Benefit
The biggest	You get the best deal from our market leverage
A clever web system	You get 24/7 access
A strong parent	You get the security of dealing with a strong and stable financial company
Employer of choice	You get highly motivated and productive employees working on your projects
150 years experience	You get cost effective and proven methods
Account executives not salesmen	You get people who understand your business, not just understand their products

Another way to use less bullet points is to use words in text boxes. Using lines and shapes with the text boxes, makes it easier to show grouping of information and logic. Again, like Jon Moon's Words in Tables, using these techniques makes your message clearer, shows the message structure and can make your message stand out. In Adam Cooper's book, *PowerPoint® presentations that sell* (2009), every page is filled with examples of persuasive layouts. (Also, It's packed with tips to create persuasive layouts, faster.) A simple example of the power of his approach is shown below.

Use text boxes	**Benefits**
Line them up	More interesting
Group them	Can show logic
Use lines to show groups	Can show complex arguments

Keep the structure simple, use signposts, keep each slide simple and use effects rarely and only for impact. Remember, PowerPoint® is just a tool.

Insight 46
Portable Persuading

"Explore your higher latitudes... be a Columbus to whole new continents and worlds within you, open new channels, not of trade but of thought."

Henry David Thoreau

Persuading, without the luxury of ducking back to the office to pick up that USB that you forgot, presents considerable challenges. These tips are from our experience persuading in places such as Port Moresby, Chicago, London and Hong Kong.

Compatibility and Data Projectors

Before you leave for a presentation off-site, or overseas, check whether your computer will be compatible with the available system. As soon as you can, confirm compatibility because some laptops and data projectors are not compatible. If you are unfamiliar with the equipment, especially the data projector, arrive early. Some projectors need to be connected before booting up your computer, while others need to be connected after booting up your computer. Also, beware, because sometimes a screensaver will cut off the signal to the projector and you will need to start again. Once you have opened your presentation, check through your presentation to make sure the data projector has not distorted your fonts.

Normally Networked

Many companies have their computers networked. Make sure that any links or files in your presentation refer to your laptop and not to a file back on the home network. In the office, disconnect your network cable and run your presentation.

That beautiful video or picture will not impress your audience if all they see is an error message telling them you left it on the office network.

Turn off the screensaver settings on the computer. A funny screensaver that everyone in the office enjoys might ruin your polished and professional persuasion.

Some companies have some laptops that are loaned to people who occasionally present outside the office. Check carefully that you have all the passwords and all the software you need. Again we suggest that you run through the presentation with the laptop disconnected from the office network.

External Power

Try to avoid presenting on battery power. Your persuasion Is too important for a battery failure to interrupt. If possible, ring ahead to confirm you will have access to an external power source. When the only option is running your presentations from batteries, check your battery power is enough and charge your notebook before your presentation. Start your computer before you enter the presentation and put it into sleep mode (or hibernation or standby). Then, when you are ready to present, in a few moments you can activate your presentation. There are ways to minimise the risk of technical problems, but in locations outside major cities, always carry your own extension cord and power pack.

Position... position

Position yourself and the computer, so your audience has a clear line of sight. If you are using a data projector, use a cordless mouse or remote presenter to run the presentation. So, you can sit apart from the computer and you are better able to gauge audience reaction and encourage participation.

Avoid using the mouse as a pointer. Rather, if you are using a data projector, use a pen or laser pointer to point at the data screen directly. If you are presenting using the notebook screen, consider using a small pointer because sometimes it is too awkward to use the mouse.

Speakers

If your presentation includes any video or audio content, do not rely on the built in speakers in your notebook computer. Bring some small external speakers with you.

The Future

Not so long ago, the most effective form of presentation was a professionally made and edited 7–10 minute video. Corporate presentations have advanced in the past 5 years. With the increases in portable computing power and advances in software, many businesses can create their own professional looking presentations.

Today PowerPoint® animations and graphics have become an essential part of every presenter's kit. However, PowerPoint® can only take you so far.

Digital video is now surprisingly easy to incorporate into presentations. A digital video can be used to show a product in action, testimonials from customers, project messages, add movement and visual displays. New software extends far beyond the animation and graphic capabilities of software such as PowerPoint®.

The Internet offers the capability to take your digital video and sales presentation live to any audience on the planet. With the **m-space** presentation system, you can build your presentation on your local notebook then 'publish' it within minutes to a dedicated web address where your clients can access it. You can then make a conference call to your clients anywhere in the world and step them through your presentation as if you were there in the room with them. Peter Houghton, Director of Interactive Thinking, calls it 'building locally and presenting globally'. With the appropriate software, you can present on the web in a videoconference, and you can see the audience's reaction too.

There are many forms of technology, making conferencing easier and cheaper. Adobe Connect allows you to share presentations and documents while you explain them. There are many other ways of creating webinars that combine slide with telephone calls. Skype is free and allows multi-party teleconferences and one-to-one video conferences. Also, you can easily share files and there are many add-ins make conferencing easier or to record your conference.

The impact of the iPad

An important piece of technology affecting persuasion is the iPad. For small audiences, the iPad can display high-quality video with high-quality sound. Compared to a data projector, or even a laptop, the iPad's simplicity and size make it a powerful tool to persuade.

At the moment, presentations can only be shown in Apple's Keynote presentation software. You cannot show PowerPoint® presentations unless you change the format, for example to a flash movie. Given the pervasiveness of PowerPoint®, it seems certain there will soon be an app (application) to show PowerPoint® in it's native format.

Anyone serious about persuading small groups must examine the iPad and how it can help them Persuade For Results.

In the next section, we consider the impact of persuasion on company strategy and suggest how a company can keep up with changes in technology.

Section 6
Managing the Business of Persuasion

A person with an opinion and no data is just
another person with an opinion.

Insight 47
Costs

"An investment in knowledge pays the best interest!"

Benjamin Franklin

We now begin to examine issues for businesses with many presenters. What is it costing you to present and persuade? Some people would simply add together the costs of the software and call that the cost. But, let us consider the business of persuasion:

How many hours does a typical presenter take to compile a presentation?	
How many presentations does each person give per year?	
How long are the presentations?	
How many people are giving presentations?	
How much does each hour cost? (If you are not sure, use $100 as an estimate)	

With this information, we can assess whether there are opportunities to reduce costs. Let us use a real example. A company dealing in consumer goods answered the questions this way: 8 hours or more to prepare each presentation, 20 presentations/year per person, 50 people are presenting and we will assume $100/hour. The cost of preparation each year is:

$$8 \times 20 \times 50 \times 100 = \$800,000 \text{ / year.}$$

We suspect that many managers will be amazed at the costs associated with presentations. So what can a business do to reduce preparation and presentation costs? There are at least three solutions: use a library, technology and training.

Technology solutions allow presenters to choose from a library of standard slides and videos and we will discuss one of these below. PowerPoint® dominates the market for presentation software but is not yet designed to efficiently distribute and control presentations on a large scale.

When considering a library, to Persuade For Results, you need to tailor each presentation to each client. We do not support a library of standard presentations without any flexibility to modify a presentation to suit a client. However, a system which allows access to presentations to compare with see how others presented to certain clients is valuable. Also, if the business uses television advertising or produces high quality videos then, a library of these high-quality videos can have a big impact with your client.

Technology such as the **m-space** at www.info-onscreen.com.au has been designed to create presentations just like PowerPoint®, using libraries of high quality videos and slides. We will discuss this further when we consider control of presentation material. Other presentation software might also be appropriate.

On a smaller scale, individuals and smaller businesses can use solutions like Slide Executive to improve productivity (http://www.slideexecutive.com)

When persuading on complex business issues, some of the ideas developed by McKinsey are available in software called Solo™ at www.axoninc.com. Solo™ is designed for businesses like consultancies that have a team of people working on a problem, businesses who want to plan and draft concise, effective high-standard presentations and reports. We like their idea of a 'visual vocabulary' for ideas and charts, which is based on the work of Gene Zelazny. In summary, if preparation costs are high we encourage you to consider technology solutions as well as PowerPoint®.

Technology is one solution, but it will not make a difference unless the presenters know how to use the technology. Part of the reason we have made the tools in this book simple is that we want readers to be able to use them immediately, to advance skills rapidly. However, if a company has complex technology, it will have to invest in training.

Insight 48
Control

"If it is to be, it is up to me."

Joel Weldon

For reasons of governance and branding, some businesses need to control the information used to persuade. Typically, governance issues arise where the business operates in a highly regulated industry, such as pharmaceuticals or financial services. However many larger businesses in other sectors need to be concerned about trade practices legislation, anti-trust or monopolies commissions and many other business and legal issues.

Other companies, particularly with a strong brand, simply want to control presentations to ensure diverse styles of presentations do not dilute the company brand. Typically marketing departments spend large sums of money to ensure the visual image of the brand is consistent with the values of the brand. If each presenter uses different versions of the logo and different backgrounds and fonts, this confuses and dilutes the brand. Control is also important if the previous insight has shown the cost of preparation is high in your business.

Some businesses implement standard presentations and standard libraries. However as we have highlighted, different audiences need different presentations. So, this may be an efficient solution but is it effective? Can the presenters persuade for results with standard solutions?

Again, technology can help. m-space, mentioned in the previous insight, can help solve many of these problems. It can create standard libraries and allow customising of certain slides. For example, m-space can automatically download current versions of slides or videos via a network or the Internet. This helps with fast and effective updating. It also helps ensure that a presenter does not use out of date templates.

This software can also provide data on which slides have been used, how often and when. This provides information on which slides are used most and least often. Perhaps, this will help businesses design more effective and persuasive visuals. The software can also provide data about individual presenters, such as how many presentations they have given, and on what date they presented. This data allows a business to see who the most productive presenters are.

The data also allows businesses to begin to manage the productivity of their presenters and reduce the costs of presentations. This solution can be implemented as a stand-alone system to fully networked versions, with workflows and administration. If the cost of presentations is high or your business needs control for legislation, regulation or branding then this kind of solution can help. Many pharmaceutical, telecommunications, television and consumer goods businesses have invested in this technology, for example Diageo and Pfizer.

Insight 49
Business Strategy and Persuasion

*"People don't buy products or services;
they buy SOLUTIONS to their problems."*

Ted Levitt

The word strategy is often misused and misunderstood. When we use the word we mean the simple definition used by the McKinsey consultant Kenichi Omhae, who describes strategy as the intersection of three groups: customers, competitors and the company.

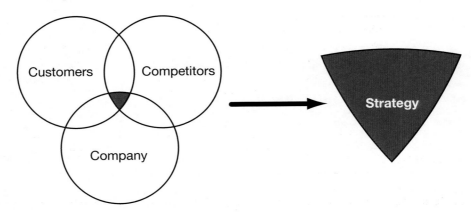

This simple definition helps when we are talking with clients about complex issues that may or may not be strategic. Our quick mental check is 'does this involve customers and competitors as well as the company?' If it does not then it is not a strategic issue.

Strategy is all about gaining and sustaining competitive advantage over your competitors to win business from customers. However, the pace of business is accelerating and Richard D'aveni argues in *Hypercompetition* that no organisation can build a competitive advantage that is sustainable. Shona Brown and Kathleen Eisenhardt, in *Competing on the Edge* suggest that Rule One of competing is, 'Advantage is only temporary'. Brown and Eisenhardt identify that different industries have a different pace, a different rhythm, while Jeffrey Williams suggests competitive advantage erodes at difference paces for each different industry.

PACE	EXAMPLES	COMMENTS	CRITICAL SUCCESS FACTORS
Slow cycle	Medical appliances.	Companies strongly shielded from competition by patents, or complex buyer-supplier relationships or strong brands.	Nurture protected markets. Isolate firm from rivals.
Standard cycle	Passenger cars, household refrigerators, electric lamps and fast food.	Products typically standardised for production at high volumes. E.g. cars and household appliances. Organisations tend to be mass market and market share oriented.	Economies of scale, market share, market control, build brand loyalty.
Fast cycle	Mobile phones, Discmans and microwave ovens.	Products tend to be based on concept, technology, or idea. Once commercialised these products do not require complex organisations to support them.	Market timing and intelligence, speed, extract temporary profits.

Jeffrey R. Williams, *How sustainable is your competitive advantage?* California Management Review, Spring 1992, pp 29–51.

This evidence tells us we need to find ways of sustaining competitive advantages and building new advantages. Certainly, persuasion is more important in some industries than others. Persuasion is important where a company makes many presentations a year to win business or where a company makes a few presentations and these have a high impact or high sales value for the company.

	LOW	HIGH
HIGH	Make presentations effective	Make presentations effective & efficient
LOW		Make presentations efficient

Impact on Company

LOW   HIGH

Number of presentations/year

We will now discuss customers and competitors. Across all industries, customers are persuaded more by visuals and involvement in a presentation.

More persuasive →

Written words	Spoken words	Still pictures	Moving pictures	Video	Interactive moving pictures and video

With improved technology and declines in price, even small companies can create presentations that are as impressive as those given by large companies. A more persuasive presentation will not give a company more capital or bigger facilities. However, it may persuade the customer to give them a chance. Malcolm Gladwell, in his book *The Tipping Point* describes how there is a point at which a small change can make a big difference. Perhaps a competitor now has the momentum to gain market share quickly.

What should you do? We suggest you experiment with some of the new presentation technology and experiment with potential alternative strategies for your business. Use the approach recommended by Shona Brown and Kathleen Eisenhardt and experiment with small, fast, low-cost trials of new technology.

No one knows exactly how technology will affect business strategy and the work of any presenter in the future. To get better at Persuading For Results, our advice is: for now, focus on building your skills and understanding the tools of persuasion; for the future, monitor your competitors, experiment with the new technology and Improve your persuasion skills.

Au revoir

All the strength you need to achieve anything is within you. Don't wait for a light at the end of the tunnel. Stride down there and light it yourself!

Sara Henderson

In this book, we wanted to fast-track your journey to being more effective when you are Persuading for Results. We shared the most up-to-date research and shared our knowledge and skills gained during several decades of persuading around the world.

We encourage you to use the tools in this book until the process becomes instinctive. However, we recognize each person will use this book in a different way and we look forward to hearing how some of you have used our suggestions.

By introducing a new way of thinking about persuasion—emphasizing the importance of the audience, focusing on action outcomes, and balancing content and style—we hope we have given you a fresh way to persuade for results. We hope you will use this book as a springboard to future success. By now it should be obvious: if you want to be more effective at persuading for results, you must become a persuasive presenter.

If we can help with personal coaching or workshops please let us know. We wish you well on your journey.

Bibliography

"When the student is ready, the teacher will appear."

Chinese Proverb

Bibliography

The references below are excellent. If you wish to pursue your own research influencing and persuasion, start with the recommended reading list. The Bibliography provides a more extensive list.

Recommended Reading

Persuasion

Cialdini, R. B. (2008), *Influence, Science and Practice*, 5 Ed, Allyn and Bacon.

Cialdini, R. Goldstein, N. and Martin, S. (2007), *YES! 50 secrets from the science of persuasion*, Profile Books.

Fisher, R. & Sharp, A (1998), *Getting it done; How to lead when you're not in charge*, Harper.

Heiman, S. E., Miller, R. & Tuleja, T. (2005), *The New Strategic Selling*, Warner Books.

Knight, S. (2010), *NLP at Work*, 3 Ed, Nicholas Brearley.

Miller, R. B., Heiman, S. E. & Tuleja, T. (2005), *Conceptual Selling*, Warner Books.

Patterson, K. Patterson, J. McMillan, R. and Switzler, A. (2002), *Crucial Conversations: Tools for talking when stakes are high*, McGraw Hill.

Rackham, N. (1996), *The SPIN Selling Fieldbook*, McGraw Hill.

Read, N. & Bistritz, S. (2009), *Selling to the C-Suite; what every executive wants you to know about successfully selling to the top*, McGraw Hill.

Tieger, P. & Barron-Tieger, B. (1998), *The Art of Speed Reading People; How to Size People Up and Speak Their Language*, Little, Brown & Company.

Whitmore, J. (2009), *Coaching for Performance*, 4 Ed, Nicholas Brearley.

More persuasive visuals

Abela, A. (2008), *Advanced Presentations by Design; Creating Communication That Drives Action*, Pfeiffer.

Cooper, A. (2009), *Powerpoint Presentations That Sell*, McGrath Hill.

Duarte, N. (2008), Slide*: ology: The Art and Science of Creating Great Presentations*, O'Reilly Media Inc.

Moon, J. (2009), *How to make an IMPACT: influence, inform and impress with your reports, presentations, business documents, charts and graphs*, FT Press.

Parker, R. (2006), *Looking Good in Print*, 6 Ed, Paraglyph.

Reynolds, G. (2008), *Presentation Zen: Simple Ideas on Presentation Design and Delivery*, New Riders.

Roam, D. (2009), *Unfolding the Napkin: The hands-On method for Solving Complex Problems with Simple Pictures*, Portfolio Trade.

Sibbet, D. (2010), *Visual Meetings: How Graphics, Sticky Notes and Idea Mapping Can Transform Group Productivity*, John Wiley & Sons.

Zelazny, G. (2006), *Say It With Charts Complete Toolkit*, McGraw Hill.

Persuading & Managing change

Black, J. S. & Gregerson, H. B. (2003), *Leading Strategic Change*, Financial Times-Prentice Hall.

Feldman, M. L. & Spratt, M. F. (2001), *Five Frogs on a Log: a CEO's field guide to accelerating the transition in mergers, acquisitions and gut wrenching change*, Wiley.

Fisher, R. & Sharp, A. (1998), *Getting it Done*, Harper.

Jackson, P. Z. & McKergow, M. (2006), *The Solutions Focus*, 2 Ed Nicholas Brearley.

Stace, D. & Dunphy, D. (2001), *Beyond the Boundaries*, 2 Ed, McGraw Hill.

Persuading with stories

Duarte, N.(2010) *Resonate: Present Visual Stories that Transform Audiences*, John Wiley & Sons.

Heath, C. and Heath, D. (2007), *Made to stick, why some ideas survive and others die*, Random House.

Strategy

Baghai, S, Coley, S. & White D. (1999), The Alchemy of Growth: Kickstarting and sustaining growth in your company, Orion Business.

Brown, S. L. & Eisenhardt, K. M. (1998), *Competing on the Edge*, Harvard Business School Press.

Grundy, T. & Brown, L. (2002), *Be Your Own Strategy Consultant*, Thomson Learning.

Kim, C. & Mauborgne, R. (2005), Blue Ocean Strategy; *How to Create Uncontested Market Space and Make the Competition Irrelevant*, Harvard Business School Press.

McGrath, R. G., Macmillan, I. C., Market Busters: 40 Strategic Moves that Drive Exceptional Business Growth, Harvard Business School press, 2005

Simons, R.,(2010), Seven Strategy Questions: a simple approach for better execution, Harvard Business Review Press.

Reference List

Accel Team. (1985), *Speaking with Confidence*, ACCEL Communications, New York City.

Adams, S. (1996), *The Dilbert Principle*, Harper Business.

Amram, M. (2002), *Value Sweep: Mapping Growth Opportunities Across Assets*, Harvard Business School Press.

Aristotle. (1991), *The Art of Rhetoric*, Penguin Books.

Armstrong, T. (1999), *7 Kinds of Smart*, Plume Books.

Baghai, Coley & White (1999), *The Alchemy of Growth*, Perseus Books.

Bailey, E. P. (1992), *A Practical Guide for Business Speaking*, Oxford University Press.

Barthes, R. (1964*), Elements of Semiology*, Hill and Wang.

Bernstein, Peter L. (1996), Against The gods, The Remarkable Story of Risk, John Wiley & Sons, Inc.

Bishop, S. (1997), *The Complete Guide to People Skills*, Gower.

Blanchard, K. & Johnson, S. (1981) *The One Minute Manager*, William Morrow & Company Inc.

Booher, D. (1994), *Communicate with Confidence*, McGraw-Hill Inc.

Bowman, D. P. (1998), *Critical Skills for Your Business Presentations*, Adams Media Corporation.

Carter, R. (1996) *Working with computer type: Colour and type*, Rotovision.

Casilone, J. A. & Thomas. (2002), A. R, *Global Manifest Destiny*, Dearborn trade Publishing.

Caslione, John & kotler, Philip (2009) *Chaotics, The business of managing and Marketing in the Age of Turbulence*, Amcom.

Cherniss, C. and Adler, M. (2000), *Promoting Emotional Intelligence in Organisations*, American Society for Training and Development.

Cialdini, R. B. (2008), *Influence, Science and Practice*, 5 Ed, Allyn and Bacon.

Clason, G. S. (1991), *The Richest Man in Babylon*, A Signet Book.

Conger, J. A. (1998), *Winning 'em Over: A New Model for Managing in the Age of Persuasion*, Simon & Schuster.

Conger, Jay A. (1998), "The Necessary Art of Persuasion", *Harvard Business Review*, May, 84–92.

Courtney, H. (2001), *20/20 Foresight, Crafting Strategy in an Uncertain World*, Harvard Business Press.

Covey, S. R. *The 7 Habits of Highly Effective People,* The Business Library.

D'Aveni, R. A. (1994), *Hypercompetition*, Free Press.

Darwin, Charles. (1854) *On the Origin of Species*, John Murray, UK.

Drew, J. (1994), *Mastering Meetings*, McGraw-Hill.

Edelman, S. (2006), *Change Your Thinking*, Da Capo Press.

Ekeren, G. V. (1988), *The Speaker's Sourcebook*, Prentice Hall.

Ekeren, G. V. (1994), *Speaker's Sourcebook II*, Prentice Hall.

Feldman, M. L. & Spratt, M. F. (2001), *Five frogs on a log, a CEO's field guide to accelerating the transition in mergers, acquisitions and gut wrenching change*, Wiley

Fisher, R. & Sharp, A (1998), *Getting it done; How to lead when you're not in charge*, Harper.

Fleming, C. (1992), *The Sound of Your Voice*, Audioworks, audiocassette.

Frankl, V. E. *Man's Search for Meaning,* Washington Square Press.

Gladwell, M. (2000), *The Tipping Point*, Abacus.

Goleman, D. (1998), *Working with Emotional Intelligence,* Bloomsbury Publishing.

Green, R. E. (1984), *The persuasive properties of color*, Media Horizons, Inc.

Guilfoyle, D. (2002), *The Charisma Effect*, McGraw-Hill Australia.

Handford, S. A. (1954) *Fables of Aesop*, Penguin Books.

Heiman, S. E., Miller, R. & Tuleja, T. (2005), *The New Strategic Selling*, Warner Books.

Henderson, R. & McAlister, M. (1998), *Be Seen Get Known Move Ahead*, Networking to Win.

Hanninger, M. (2007) *The Hidden Web*; Finding Quality Information on the Net, 2 Ed, University of New South Wales Press.

Heath, C. and Heath D. (2007), *Made To Stick, Why some ideas survive and others die*, Random House.

Hindle, T. (1999), *Making Presentations*, London: Dorling Kindersley.

Holtz, H. (1985), *Speaking for Profit*, John Wiley & Sons.

Honey, P. (1990), *Face to Face skills*, Gower.

Jenkins, A., Elder D., & Thomas, D. (1999) *How to Sell With a Laptop: Shoulder to Shoulder Techniques for Powerful Laptop Sales Presentations*, McGraw-Hill.

Jones, Gerald E. (1995), *How To Lie With Charts*, Sybex.

Jung, C. G. and von Franz, M.-L. (1964), *Man and His Symbols*, Aldus Books Ltd.

Jung, C. G. (1971), *Psychological Types*, Princeton University Press.

Kaplan, R. S. and Norton, D. P (2001), *The Strategy-focused Organisation*, Harvard Business School Press.

Kaplan, R. S. and Norton, D. P (2004), *Strategy Maps*, Harvard Business School Press.

Kaye, M. (1994), *Communication Management*, Prentice Hall.

Kirby, T. (1986), *117 Ideas for better Business Presentations*, ECTN, Winter Park.

Kliem, R. & Ludin, I. (1995). *Stand and Deliver*, Gower.

Knight, S. (2010), *NLP at Work*, 3 Ed, Nicholas Brearley.

Kupsh, J. (1995), *Create High-Impact Business Reports*, NTC Learning Works.

LaHaye, T. (1988), *Why You Act the Way You Do*, Living Books, Tyndale House Publishers.

Leech, T. (1993), *How To Prepare, Stage, & Deliver Winning Presentations*, Amacom.

Lewis, R. (1969), *Audiovisual Handbook*, Toastmasters International, USA.

Mackay, H. *Why Don't People Listen*, Pan Australia.

Malouf, D. (1988), *Confidence Through Public Speaking*, Information Australia.

Malouf, D. (1988), *How to Create and Deliver a Dynamic Presentation*, Simon & Schuster.

Mandel, S. (1987), *Effective Presentation Skills*, Crisp Publications.

Mandela, N. R. (1994), *Long walk To Freedom*, Abacus.

Marston, W. M. (1987), *Emotions of Normal People*, Performax Systems International, Inc.

McCallister, L. (1994), *I Wish I'd Said That!*, John Wiley & Sons.

Metcalf, F. (1986), *The Penguin Dictionary of Modern Humorous Quotations*, Penguin Books.

Millbower. (2000), *Training With a Beat*, Kogan Page Limited, London.

Miller, R. B., Heiman, S. E. & Tuleja, T. (2005), *Conceptual Selling*, Warner Books.

Mollison, B. (1991), *Introduction to Permaculture*, Tagari Publications.

Moon, J. (2009), How to make an Impact: Influence, Inform

Morgan, G. (1997), *Images of Organisations*, 2 Ed, Sage.

Morgan, G. (1997), *Imaginization: New mindsets for seeing, organising and managing*, Sage.

Morgan, N. (2001), "The Kinesthetic Speaker: Putting Action into Words". In *Harvard Business Review*, April, 112–120.

Morrison, T., Conaway, W., & Borden, G. (1994), *Kiss, Bow, or Shake Hands*, Adams Media Corporation.

Munter, M. (2008), *Guide to Managerial Communication*, 8 Ed, Prentice Hall.

Musashi, M. (1993), *The Book of Five Rings*, Barnes & Noble Books.

Ohmae, K. (1991), *The Mind of a Strategist*, McGraw Hill.

Nomchong, D (2011) Leukaemia: a minor inconvenience, Braidwood Publishing.

Parker, R. C. (2006), *Looking Good in Print*, 6 Ed, Paraglyph.

Pease, A. & Pease B. (1998), *Why Men Don't Listen & Women Can't Read Maps*, Pease Training International.

Peoples, D. A. (1992), *Presentations Plus*, John Wiley & Sons.

Price Bowman, D. (1998), *Presentations*, Adams Media Corporation.

Rackham, N. (1996), *The SPIN Selling Fieldbook*, McGraw Hill.

Rasiel, E. M. (1999), *The McKinsey Way*, McGraw Hill.

Reivich, K. & Shatté, A. (2002) *The Resilience Factor,* Three Rivers Press.

Richardson, L. (1990), *Winning Group Sales Presentations: A Guide to Closing the Deal*, Irwin.

Russo, J. E. & Schoemaker, P. J. H. (2002), *Winning Decisions*, Piatkus.

Scannell, E. & Newstrom, J. (1980) *Games Trainers Play,* McGraw Hill.

Scannell, E. & Newstrom, J. (1994) *Even More Games Trainers Play,* McGraw Hill.

Seligman, M. (2006), *Learned Optimism*, Vintage.

Shannon, C. & Weaver, W. (1949) *Mathematical Model of Communication*, Bell System Technical Journal.

Simmons, A. (2001), *The Story factor, Inspiration, influence and persuasion through the art of storytelling*, Perseus Publishing.

Simpson, J. B. (1988), *Simpson's Contemporary Quotations*, Houghton Mifflin Company.

Skovgard, R. O. (1984), *Openings: A selection of opening statements from recent speeches by executives*, The Executive Speaker.

Smith, D.(1993), *Powerful Presentation Skills*, Career Track Publications, Colorado, USA.

Sperber, D. & Wilson, D. (1996), *Relevance—Communication and Cognition*, Blackwell.

Spicer, K. (1985), *Think On Your Feet*, Doubleday Canada.

Spinrad, L. & T. (1997), *Speaker's Lifetime Library*, Prentice Hall.

Straker, D. *Rapid Problem Solving*, Gower.

Straw, J (2002), *The 4-Dimensional Manager*, Berrett-Koehler.

Suzuki, D. (1999), *Naked Ape to Superspecies,* Allen and Unwin.

Tannen, D. (1995), "The Power of Talk: Who Gets Heard and Why". In *Harvard Business Review*, Sep–Oct.

Tannen, Deborah, *You just don't Understand—Women and Men in Conversation,* Virago Press.

The 3M Management Team with Jeannine Drew. (1994), *Mastering Meetings: Discovering the Hidden Potential of Effective Business Meetings*.

The 3M Management Team. (1987), *How to Run Better Business Meetings,* McGraw-Hill Inc.

Tieger, P. D & Barron-Tieger, B. (1995), *Do What You Are*, 2 Ed., Little, Brown and Company.

Tieger, P. D & Barron-Tieger, B. *The Art of Speedreading people*, Little, Brown and Company.

Walkowski, D. (2000), *Visio 2000 for Dummies*, Wiley.

Warr, P, Editor. (1996), *Psychology at Work,* Penguin.

Weissman, J (2003) *Presenting to Win, The Art of telling your story*, Prentice Hall.

Whitmore, J. (2009), *Coaching for Performance*, 4 Ed, Nicholas Brearley.

Williams, J. R. (1992), 'How sustainable is your competitive advantage?' *California Management Review*, Spring, pp 29–51.

Zelazny, G. (2006), *Say It With Charts Complete Toolkit*, McGraw Hill.

The Persuader's Toolkit

"You can discover more about a person in an hour of play than in a year of conversation."

Plato

FRAMING TOOL

Ideas: Consider at least two different frames	
What does the frame highlight:	
What is in the shadows of the frame:	
Comparisons — what are the differences	

How can I frame to emphasise...	**EMPHASISE GAINS**	**MINIMISE LOSSES**

CREATING A PERSUASIVE MESSAGE USING THE SIX TOOLS:

Tool	How could you apply these to persuade the target?
Like People like people who are like them. Look for similarities.	
Reciprocity People feel obliged to repay gifts and favours.	
Social Proof People follow the lead of other similar people. Use peer power when you can.	
Consistency People align their behaviour with small commitments. Make their commitments active, public and voluntary.	
Authority People defer to experts. Expose your expertise; do not assume it is self-evident.	
Scarcity People want more of what they can have less of. Highlight unique benefits and exclusive information.	

OBJECTIVE	TASKS	DATE
Arrange the logistics		
Understand Audience		
Research Data		
Write Close		
Write Opening		
Structure Contents		
Questions		
Follow up		
Visuals		
Handouts		

PLANNING TOOL	
Presentation Topic	
Date	
Time	
Location	
Coordinator and contact number	
What prompted the request for your presentation?	
Number of Attendees	
Who is your audience?	
Who will be speaking before and after you?	
Will the context be formal or informal?	
What are the goals of the presentation?	
What are your main points?	
What facilities will you have access to?	
What organisation will be required (flights, accommodation, catering)?	

AUDIENCE RESEARCH TOOL

Who is in your audience? Who are the key members?	
What is their motivation for attending?	
How are they related to your topic?	
What do they know about you? What do they need to know?	
What is their current knowledge of the topic?	
What do they want / need to know?	
What is the audience's attitude to you and your topic?	
How do you expect the audience to react to your presentation?	
What techniques would be best for this audience?	
What are the demographics of the audience? (Age, occupation, religion, socioeconomic status, gender, education, political background, etc)	
What are your research findings relating to the industry / company background?	
How will you follow up your presentation?	

FAST ANALYSIS OF YOUR PERSUASION TARGET TOOL

How they prefer to communicate:

Talks more than listens ☐   Listens more than talks ☐

How fast they talk:

Fast-paced ☐   Slow-paced ☐

How they prefer information:

Details ☐   Big Picture ☐

How they decide by focusing on:

Tasks (& facts) ☐   People (& Feelings) ☐

RESEARCHING THE DATA TOOL

What are the key books relating to your topic?	
What are some relevant journals to use as a resource?	
What are some web sites that you should look at?	
Is there someone in particular that you should interview for information?	
Do you have any existing notes on the topic?	
Are there any other sources that you think could be useful?	

THE CLOSE TOOL

Duration	
How will you signal your close?	
How will you summarise your main points?	
What is your 'statement of reality'?	
What action is required from the audience?	
How will you close with impact?	

THE OPENING TOOL

Presentation title	
Duration	
How will you 'set the scene' for the audience arrival? (Music, picture, beverages available, meet and greet.)	
Who will introduce you? How will they do this?	
How will you connect with the audience?	
How will you create an action focus?	
What is your benefit statement?	
How will you give the audience a sneak preview of what's to come?	

THE CONTENT TOOL

Duration:	
What is your main objective?	
What action do you want the audience to take?	
What content model will you use?	

KEY POINTS	TIMING	RESOURCES
PAST		
Q & A		
PRESENT		
Q & A		
FUTURE		
FINAL Q & A		

QUESTION TIME TOOL

How long will you allow for questions?	
Will you allow questions to be asked as you go or only at the end?	
How will you open the questions? How will you encourage people to talk?	
What questions do you anticipate the audience will ask?	
What are your responses to these questions?	
How will you respond to irrelevant questions?	
What is your strategy for responding to questions that you do not know the answer to?	
How will you close the question time?	

VISUALS TOOL

Projector	
Screen — size/height	
Quality of Projection	
Where are the light switches	
Will the lights be on or off?	
What graphics will you use?	
Background colours/effects	
Slide Animation	
Slide Transition	
Proof read for typing errors	
What font will you use?	
Will you use bullets?	

COLOUR TOOL

Is there a colour commonly identified with the mood you wish to create?	
Is there a colour with a logical link to the content or substance?	
Do you want to use this colour as your base?	
Identify the main colour you wish to use.	
Identify two other colours that will work well with your main colour.	
Decide on one colour for all headings.	
Use a different shade of that same colour for sub-headings, or a different colour entirely?	
Do you wish to link to company colours or company brand?	
Impression created	
Link to company colours?	
Less than 3 colours per slide?	
Do your colours look good once projected onto a screen?	

INVOLVE THE AUDIENCE TOOL

How can I use imagery?	
What questions can I ask?	
How can I use quotations?	
How can I help the audience visualise?	
How can I use surprise gifts?	
How can I build activity into the presentation?	

HANDOUTS TOOL

Are they a summary or supplementary?	
Are they interactive working notes?	
Timing of distribution	
Include statistics or just insights?	
Include articles or case studies?	
Magazine articles?	
Will you include your presentation slides?	
Will you allow flicking time at start?	
Will you allow room to write?	
Will you include graphics?	
Will you use helpers to distribute?	
How many pages will you include?	

DELIVERING BAD NEWS TOOL

How will you warn the audience that you have bad news?	
How will you word the negative message?	
How do you intend to identify with the audience?	
What is your strategy for diffusing audience anger?	
What are some positive aspects of the message?	
What action plan will you propose for dealing with the bad event?	
Will you consult with someone else regarding this issue?	
Would the news be better delivered from someone else, and if so, who?	

LOCATION TOOL

Location	
Size	
Temperature	
Ventilation	
Lighting	
Distractions	
Contact for equipment problems	
Emergency phone	

FACILITIES TOOL

Stereo or mono (two or one) projectors?	
Theatre	
U-shape	
Boardroom	
Cabaret	
Classroom	
Location extra paper and pens	

"The greatest discovery of my age is that men can change their circumstances by changing the attitude of their mind."

William James